Historical Truth and Lies about the Past

Historical Truth

The

University

of North

Carolina

Press

Chapel Hill

& London

and *Lies* about the Past

Reflections

on Dewey,

Dreyfus,

de Man,

and

Reagan

Alan B. Spitzer

© 1996 The University of North Carolina Press
All rights reserved
Manufactured in the United States of America

A portion of this book appeared in a slightly
different form in "John Dewey, the Trial of Leon
Trotsky, and the Search for Historical Truth," *History
and Theory* 29, no. 1 (1990): 16–37, and is reprinted
with the permission of the publisher.

The paper in this book meets the guidelines for
permanence and durability of the Committee on
Production Guidelines for Book Longevity of the
Council on Library Resources.

Library of Congress Cataloging-in-Publication Data
Spitzer, Alan B. (Alan Barrie), 1925–
Historical truth and lies about the past: reflections
on Dewey, Dreyfus, de Man, and Reagan / Alan B.
Spitzer.
p. cm.   Includes bibliographical references (p.   )
and index. Contents: Introduction : historical
argument when the political chips are down—John
Dewey, the "trial" of Leon Trotsky, and the search
for historical truth—Versions of truth in the Dreyfus
case—The debate over the wartime writings of Paul
de Man—Ronald Reagan's Bitburg narrative.
ISBN 0-8078-2289-2. — ISBN 0-8078-4598-1 (pbk.)
1. Historiography. 2. Truth. 3. Objectivity. 4. History,
Modern—20th century—Case studies. I. Title.
D13.S645 1996   95-47876
                                            CIP

00 99 98 97 96   5 4 3 2 1

To the memory of Michael Brody

Contents

Acknowledgments

Portions of this manuscript were constructively criticized by Charles Hale, David Joravsky, Janet Freeman, Alan Nagel, Steven Ungar, and Robert Preyer.

I wish also to thank Lewis Bateman for his warm encouragement, Christi Stanforth for impeccable copyediting, Gretchen Bouliane for reading proof on short notice, and Steven and Nancy Reschly for help in preparing the manuscript when they had better things to do.

The resident linguist, Mary Freeman Spitzer, was indispensable throughout.

Historical Truth and Lies about the Past

Introduction

Unfortunately, if the norm of truth is driven out through the

door, it comes in again through the window.—Paul Veyne

Historical Argument When
the Political Chips Are Down

Although the "whole concept of historical truth" has been called into question,[1] almost everyone claims to know what a lie about the past looks like.[2] In
historical debate, lying falls at the near end of a spectrum ranging from willful
to unwitting misrepresentation, from the falsification to the misinterpretation
of evidence, from arguments in manifest bad faith to well-intentioned in-
coherence. Separating out the historical chaff depends on some claim to cognitive authority, to some assumption of what John Dewey called "warranted
assertability." My concern is not to unmask certain historical lies but to argue
that the refutation of falsehood or error depends on some criteria of veracity
and validity and that these criteria are exposed in the heat of debate regardless
of the theoretical affirmation or repudiation of epistemological standards. I
intend to consider these issues in case studies that examine contradictory
histories of politically charged events.

Among the contradictions is the tendency to have things both ways. Skepticism about the authority of historical representation never seems to inhibit the
refutation of misrepresentations, especially of the recent past. Yet the presumption that historical truths are problematic applies even more to readings
of the immediate than of the distant past. Where the reconstruction of relatively recent events carries a heavy political freight, the interpretive perspective

is more colored by personal and ideological bias than are academic histories of events lost to living memory. But conflicting versions of politically loaded recent histories are rarely defended simply with reference to political loyalties. Each history claims the authority of particular truths and implicitly assumes the validity of the general criteria of truth applied to the particular claim. In fact, the higher the political and moral stakes, the more likely the antagonists are to appeal to generally warranted standards of authoritative discourse—to conventional criteria of relevant evidence and rational inference. All of which is to say that while I cannot demonstrate to you some universally valid criteria of historical truth, I can tell you what yours are.

Over the past twenty years, powerful arguments have undermined our confidence in historical objectivity, in universal standards of truth, and even in "the viability of the search for stable and determinate meanings."[3] Skepticism about the ability of any observer to represent any past with ecumenical authority is often fortified with reference to the observer's "historicity." This term is variously defined but often refers to the impossibility of establishing absolute standards for determining the truth or falsity of propositions, because such standards themselves proceed from the historical location and personal circumstances of the interpreter; from the unstated assumptions of his or her community; from the traditions that constitute the matrix of individual judgment; from the perceptual apparatus with which each person comes into the world; and from the very language with which each of us is equipped to articulate and therefore "think" these perceptions. For our purposes the issue is not so much the relative validity of particular "truths" as what has been characterized as the "historicity of the criteria of truth."[4]

Doubts about the historian's ability to represent past realities as they "really" were has a long history, distinguished in America by the names of Charles Beard and Carl Becker. Hayden White's *Metahistory: The Historical Imagination in Nineteenth-Century Europe*, first published in 1973,[5] has renewed the argument and assumed the status of a modern demiclassic even for those who disagree with it. For White, the key to understanding a historical work is in the language, which imposes a pattern of meaning and interpretation by its very structure, regardless of the epistemological argument summoned to justify a historical account. What he calls the "tropological strategy" is fundamental: the various linguistic tropes, as well as "modes" of emplotment, explanation, and ideology, define the work and in a certain sense make it incommensurable with other histories written out of other linguistic strategies. The precise degree of relativism entailed by this approach is moot, partly because one cannot find a decisive answer in White himself; but certainly some of his statements can be read as assertions of an extreme philosophic and historical relativism. For example, he was quoted in the *New York Times Book Review* as asserting, "It is possible to tell different stories about the past and there is no way, finally, to check them out against the facts of the matter, the criterion for evaluating them is moral or poetic."[6] Other historians or philosophers of history have been more categorical. For F. R. Ankersmit, "criteria of truth and falsity do not apply to historical representations of the past." According to Sande Cohen, historians "touch the objects of the discourse only by recourse to the already-meant; hence every shred of historical meaning belongs to the discourse and not to the objects."[7]

The classic objection to such arguments is that they are self-refuting—examples of the "self-excepting fallacy"[8]—not simply in the abstract but also in the specific arguments intended to undermine the authority to which they themselves appeal. Relativists who cite the failures of objectivity in historical works assume the authority of their own inference from publicly accessible evidence. The classic response to this objection has been to embrace the contradiction, to affirm that historical relativism is itself historically relative.[9]

It is, however, difficult to find anyone willing to push historical skepticism to the point of a nihilism that would put us all out of business. The motives for drawing back from the solipsistic abyss are partly pragmatic: no one wishes to relativize out of existence the arsenal of argument against deplorable—racist, sexist, and so forth—histories. Or, as Wulf Kansteiner puts it, "How can we write history successfully, for example, effectively displace unwanted emplotments of the past, without recourse to the concept of the truth?"[10]

This is not a hypothetical question. In our day it bears most directly and poignantly on the historiography of the Holocaust.[11] Hayden White, probably the most influential American subverter-from-within of the epistemological self-confidence of the historical profession, has been more or less forced on the defensive with regard to that ineluctable issue:[12]

It is often alleged that "formalists" such as myself, who hold that any historical object can sustain a number of equally plausible descriptions or narratives of its processes, effectively deny the reality of the referent, promote a debilitating relativism that permits any manipulation of the evidence as long as the account produced is structurally coherent, and thereby allow the kind of perspectivism that permits even a Nazi version of Nazism's history to claim a certain minimal credibility. Such formalists are typically confronted with questions such as the following: Do you mean to say that the occurrence and nature of the Holocaust is only a matter of opinion and that one can write its history in whatever way one pleases? Do you imply that any account of that event is as valid as any other account so long as it meets certain formal requirements of discursive practices and that one has no responsibility to the victims to tell the truth about the indignities and cruelties they suffered? Are there not certain historical events that tolerate none of that mere cleverness that allows criminals or their admirers to feign accounts of their crimes that effectively relieve them of their guilt or responsibility or even, in the worst instances, allows them to maintain that the crimes they committed never happened? In such questions we come to the bottom line of the politics of interpretation which informs not only historical studies but the human and social sciences in general.

Having posed the issue with such precision, White then rather speaks around it, approaching it by way of Pierre Vidal-Naquet's denunciation of the obscene cottage industry engaged in fabricating denials of the Holocaust's historical reality. White apparently accepts Vidal-Naquet's assertion of a factual bedrock, "a terrain of positive history [where] true opposes false quite simply, independent of any kind of an interpretation." He then qualifies this rather striking concession to the authority of the world outside the observer with this caveat: "the distinction between a lie and an error or a mistake in interpretation may be more difficult to draw with respect to historical events less amply documented than the Holocaust."

However, the essential question that White poses to historical interpretation bears not on the degree of documentation but on how it functions for the interpreter. Historical interpretations that pretend to complete objectivity or neutrality inescapably conceal a political agenda, usually favorable to the status quo: "one of the things one learns from the study of history is that such study is never innocent ideologically or otherwise, whether launched from the political perspective of the Left, the Right, or the Center." We are left, it seems, with a politically charged historical discourse constrained to some extent by the authority of those brute facts where, in Vidal-Naquet's words (quoted by White), "true opposes false quite simply, independent of any kind of interpretation."[13]

Elsewhere, in answer to such critics as Carlo Ginzburg, White argues that the conflict between competing historical narratives "has less to do with the facts of the matter in question than with the different meanings with which the facts can be endowed by emplotment." However, this comes after a considerable concession to the facts of the matter: "obviously, considered as accounts of events, already established facts, 'competing narratives' can be assessed, criticized, and ranked on the basis of their fidelity to the factual record, their comprehensiveness, and the coherence of whatever arguments they may contain."[14]

This is a familiar qualifier voiced by many of those who question historical objectivity, the correspondence theory of truth, or any version of foundationalism. In *That Noble Dream: The Objectivity Question and the American Historical Profession*, a richly documented, trenchantly argued work whose title tells all, Peter Novick demonstrates how generations of American historians have in practice violated the profession's essential ideal, or perhaps the profession's founding myth, of "objective historical truth." Yet Novick, following William James, insists, "The proposition that 'truths' are multiple and perspectival never had the corollary that there is no such thing as error or mendacity." According to Dominick LaCapra, historians "must attend to the facts, especially when they test and contest his own convictions and desires." Joan Scott sees history as "an interpretive practice, not an objective, neutral science"; but "to maintain this does not signal the abandonment of all standards; acknowledging that history is an interpretive practice does not imply that 'anything goes.'" For Allan Megill, "the argument [for the legitimacy of narrative] is not for the maxim, 'anything goes.'" Even Frank Ankersmit asserts that the historian should not misread sources and make mistakes in logic.[15] Disclaimers of this sort are expressed by many others—including postmodernist critics and philosophic pragmatists such as Richard Rorty—who do not want to be nailed to "the silly and self-refuting view that every belief is as good as every other."[16]

There does seem to be little point in attempting to refute a position that no one admits to. Still, those qualifications of historical nihilism simply return us to square one: on what grounds? By whose authority?

One answer to the problem of finding criteria that can reassure us that "anything" does not go has been to locate these criteria in some variety of an authoritative community, or an interpretive community or a community of competence, or, as Joan Scott has it, "discursive communities (in this case of historians)."[17] Actually, the standards to which she appeals—that is, a commitment to accuracy and the procedures of verification and documentation—are not techniques peculiar to historians but familiar grounds for the evaluation of arguments about the past or the present in or out of the academy.

In an essay concerned with "the effort to ground the truth of an analysis in a reference to historical context," Lynn Hunt castigates partisans in the debate over the wartime writings of Paul de Man for leaps of logic, ad hominem arguments, false analogies, and conflations of positions—"rhetorical sleights of hand" that add up to egregious misuses of historical argument. This episode reminds us, she says, that, "the discipline of a discipline, by which I mean the rules of conduct governing argument with a discipline, does have a worthy function. Such rules make a community of arguers possible."[18] Here she too evokes the rule of the discipline of history; but actually, her well-placed criticism of bad arguments appeals to standards—epistemological, logical, and ethical—that are not confined to any particular discipline.[19]

Hunt's "rules of conduct" legitimate what Allan Megill calls "disciplinary objectivity claims," which are, he remarks, "products of epistemological insecurity."[20] The insecurity is not resolved simply by locating authority in the standards of the historians' community. The criteria for the validation of specific historical claims are instances of general criteria for the truth-content of propositions of a certain sort. Therefore, they are vulnerable to skepticism regarding the absolute validity of the general criteria, but the skeptics are responsible to those standards to the extent that they appeal to them to confirm their particular claims.

In the debate over the relation between the history of the Holocaust and German national identity—the *Historikerstreit*—some German historians dismissed Jürgen Habermas's critique of their apologetics because he was not a member of the guild. "True enough," observes Charles Maier, "Habermas is not a historian—but historians have never claimed a hermetic discipline. To distort what an opponent has written violates intellectual argument in general, not just the historians' supposed reverence for text."[21]

One does not have to be a historian to take the point of Peter Novick's sardonic description of how objectivity was set aside by American historians during the various hot and cold wars of this century.[22] And to command his readers' assent Novick implicitly claimed the authority of the standards that those historians had violated. That is why David Hollinger characterized Novick's book as "a very traditional monograph attentive in the extreme to standard professional norms." Novick's response to this "left-handed compliment" was to say that one used whatever argument would convince and that when speaking to a group of historians, one used the sort of discourse that would do that particular job: "Addressing the existing historical profession, which has its privileged idiom, its rules about what makes you gain credibility and what makes you lose it, its fetishized procedures and rules of discourse, I do those things that gain me credibility and avoid those things that would make me less believable and more vulnerable—that would embarrass and intend to discredit me."[23]

There is something to this. If Novick had addressed a different audience, he might have changed his rhetoric; but despite my respect for his flinty integrity, I don't completely believe him. For example, Novick's depiction of a strain of anti-Semitism in the profession is supported by conventional procedures of documentation and inference not, I think, because he simply thought that this would fly for fellow historians but because he is convinced by what he documents. I imagine that a presentation to any other audience would have appealed to the same criteria of truth even if he delivered his conclusions in a somewhat different rhetoric. If the discipline did not respond to those standards, so much the worse for it.

One might say that Novick does frame his historical argument according to the standards of an "interpretive community," but one considerably broader than that of the membership of the American Historical Association. If, as Richard Rorty might say, one supports one's claims by appeal to one's current conceptual scheme, or the conceptual scheme of one's community,[24] that conceptual scheme and that community are defined by the specific language of the claim. This is complicated, in practice, where claims are legitimated through reference to incompatible conceptual schemes. The people who do that belong to a community willing to sacrifice conceptual consistency for a polemical payoff.

For example, those who locate the validation of certain historical claims in a reading of religious texts often justify their histories through an appeal to conventional secular standards of evidence and inference. The assumption of a miraculous suspension of natural processes may be fortified through reference to traces of natural events.

Under the heading "Despite tests, the Turin Shroud is still revered," the *New York Times* of Sunday, June 11, 1989, reported on radiocarbon tests which demonstrated that the imprint of the so-called Shroud of Turin could not have been that of the body of Jesus—that is, it could not have been his burial cloth. The answer of the pastor of Turin Cathedral, where the shroud is stored, was, "Whatever science may insist, it has had no effect at all." One can hardly argue with that affirmation; one simply rejects or accepts it. However, the *Times* cited a physicist who argued that the extraordinary event of Christ's resurrection might have radiated heat or light sufficient to have altered the cloth's nuclear composition—"That would have thrown off the radiocarbon tests"—thereby salvaging religious certainty through (temporarily unrefuted) secular conjecture.

When the assertion of infallibility is essentially secular, the authority of empirical observation and rational discourse is inevitably woven into the argument. Whether the truth-conditions for historical propositions are located in the bosom of the infallible leader, or in a myth of ethnic origin, or in the ideology of a political movement, the claims are also assumed to correspond to a reality that can be authenticated to the satisfaction of any honest and reasonable person. Stalin's dismissal of the historical "archive rats" was prima facie true but also utterly convincing—or so the Soviet citizens had better believe.

Perhaps the most common repudiation of historical objectivity in practice proceeds from a definition of truth as that which serves the cause. This premise is difficult to confront when shielded by obfuscation, as it usually is. People rarely want to state publicly that it is meet and right to lie in their good cause.[25] The apparently unexceptionable claim that "truth serves our cause" is often translated as "only that which serves the cause is true," or, even more often, "that which damages the cause cannot be true." Such tactics might be subsumed under the pragmatic standard of historical truth. Or perhaps this is vulgar pragmatism. In any case, one scarcely expects to convince through the admission of a virtuous lie.

This is especially the case where histories carry contemporary political freight. The currently popular assumption that history is essentially political or even that history is propaganda[26] doesn't tell anyone how, in principle, to relate the politics to the history, unless one is simply to enlist history in the service of a particular political line. This is to assume that historical truth is in the eye of the observer and that political right is self-evident.

For many members of my political generation, the most plausible reconstructions of certain pasts—the case of Alger Hiss, for example—were not necessarily congruent with our political preferences. To defer to the evidence that imposes a politically unpalatable conclusion is indeed to make a political decision, just as the refusal to accept as true any proposition that contravenes one's political ends is a political, and a moral, choice.

The argument that the commitment to conventional standards of historical veridicality, like all other discursive decisions, is a political commitment cannot dispense with the standards. Where the claim to historical authority is simply political, it loses the authority of the standards. The protagonists of the intensely political controversies discussed in the following chapters were acutely aware of this.

In an article in *History and Theory*, Raymond Martin proposed that philosophers of history explain, "through case studies[,] . . . the really central and apparently intractable ways in which historical studies are *more* subjective, *as a matter of fact*, than the sciences" (emphasis in original).[27] I intend to examine, through case studies, the central and intractable ways in which an appeal to conventional empirical and rational standards, and an appeal to objectivity—in the sense of the consistent application of one's own best standards for ascertaining truth, irrespective of other preferences—were required to legitimate politically charged versions of past events.

There are plenty of recent instances of the tendentious wedding of history and politics: the nationalist myths resuscitated to legitimate atrocities in the Balkans, for one example; or the histories fabricated to legitimate the peddling of anti-Semitism to black college students; or the revival of venerable histories of conspiracies allegedly committed to imposing an alien supergovernment on this nation. Above all, there are those "revisionist" histories of the Holocaust, unmatched in the cynicism of their appeals to conventional standards of historical validation. I did not think that I could usefully add to the powerful critical literature on that subject.[28] The cases that I have chosen retain a contemporary relevance and pose issues with a deep theoretical resonance as they illustrate how the cognitive authority of historical argument is enlisted in the service of political and moral agendas. They are arranged not chronologically but according to the direction of the argument.

The first of these studies will examine the response to the hearing of a commission chaired by John Dewey in Mexico City in April 1937 to allow Leon Trotsky to answer the accusations leveled against him at the Moscow Purge Trials. The manifest fabrications of the confessions implicating Trotsky led Dewey and the commission to conclude that the accusations were false in the light of "evidence and objective fact." The ferocious attacks on the Dewey Commission orchestrated by communist parties and their sympathizers ostensibly appealed to the same criteria of historical truth as those of the Dewey Commission. To affirm that the touchstone for truth was simply the party line would have been to lose all credibility in the open forum of international debate. Many fellow travelers, liberals, and antifascists engaged in complex rationalizations that were more or less pragmatic, in their concern with the divisive effects on the antifascist coalition, or hermeneutic, with reference to the historical meaning of the Soviet experiment.

We now find the Dewey Commission's conclusions more persuasive than those of Stalinists or fellow travelers or "agnostic" liberals not because of their superior tropological strategies, or their skillful parade of rhetorical figures, or the hermeneutic fusing of historical horizons, but because they satisfy familiar criteria of empirical inference and rational discourse.

My second case is the Dreyfus affair. Here I examine the criteria for historical truth affirmed by parties to a controversy in which even a neutral attitude regarding conflicting versions of past events became a political stand. Partisan Dreyfusards and anti-Dreyfusards believed in the objective, evidentially grounded validity of their respective convictions about Dreyfus's guilt or innocence. As evidence for the latter view accumulated, the thesis that Dreyfus was in fact guilty required arguments beyond conventional appeals to probative evidence.

From the beginning, the truth about the Dreyfus case was understood as inseparable from its consequences. While it was not absent from Dreyfusard rhetoric, this pragmatic criterion became an indispensable argument in the other camp and remains so in various qualifications or repudiations of standard histories of the affair. The weaker version argued during the affair was that no truth could be accepted that entailed deplorable consequences. The stronger version was that the consequences constituted the truth. As the disintegration of the high command, the weakening of the French state, and the fragmentation of the French community followed from an affirmation of Dreyfus's innocence, he must have been guilty.

A subtle addition to this line was advanced by Maurice Barrès, a clever and influential litterateur and politician. According to Barrès, truth was to be located in a given community or, generally, in a nation. There was a French truth and a Jewish truth, necessarily incommensurable and therefore beyond argument. Barrès's appeal to solidarity as the matrix of truth has a contemporary resonance, although present-day advocates of such a criterion would scarcely wish to be aligned with the Barrès version of it.

The third case follows out the controversy over the wartime writings of the late Paul de Man, an immensely influential scholar and literary theorist. Here again, I am interested in the criteria for telling the truth about the past. The focus in this chapter is not so much on lying as on the tendentious and opportunistic selection of those criteria.

The discovery of de Man's articles in collaborationist journals precipitated a remarkably bitter ad hominem controversy between critics of de Man, or of the contemporary movement, sometimes labeled deconstructionism, in which he played a signal role, and de Man's friends, admirers, and associates in that movement. I have been impressed by the extent to which the controversy's opposing parties, as well as those with mixed or nuanced opinions, have proceeded from the same assumptions regarding evidence that authoritatively represents past events. Although the implications of the evidence are vehemently disputed, the conclusions about what actually happened are unproblematic. And these "brute facts" about the past have had a significant influence on the present. At a time when there has been considerable emphasis on the way historical writing "constructs" the past, we have an example of the transformation of the present by the unanticipated evidence of past events.

Furthermore, the debate over the moral and ideological implications of de Man's past has been conducted in the language of conventional argument. Postmodernist polemicists such as Jacques Derrida, J. Hillis Miller, and Jonathan Culler accuse de Man's severe critics of inaccuracies, argument ad hominem, epistemological bad faith, and so forth. However, their attempts to dilute the effect of de Man's writings violate the standards to which they appeal and, according to some commentators on the debate, have done more harm to the reputation of deconstructionism than anything written by de Man.

The final case, entitled "Ronald Reagan's Bitburg Narrative," explores the response to mendacity—that is, telling lies about the past—in the public forum. The focus of this chapter is on President Reagan's defense of his visit to the German military cemetery where SS men were buried, cast in the form of a historical narrative that some found as offensive as the trip itself. This case has less to do with historical validity than with historical veracity. President Reagan was not engaged in theoretically undermining or affirming rational/empirical standards according to convenience but in contradictions of a different sort: his stories about the past implicitly exploited the common-sense assumption that what he said represented what actually happened, but his operational criterion was not epistemological but pragmatic: not "Is it true?" but "How will it play?"

On the one hand, I will consider whether those who assimilate criteria for historical truth to "equally legitimate narrative strategies," or who find it difficult to distinguish historical from fictional narrative, or who apply the pragmatic standard in the light of whether historical narratives "work," can establish the ground for refuting historical claims of immediate political and moral relevance embedded in the narrative. On the other hand, I will examine the rhetoric of those conservative critics of the relativist assault on the classical values of "Western civilization," including the moral commitment to truth, in the light of their support for a characteristically mendacious political regime—those for whom skepticism about objective truth in the university is a threat to civilization as we have known it, while mendacity in the office of the president is a bagatelle.

In presenting these case studies, I will argue that an appeal to the "historicity of the criteria for truth" is irrelevant when those engaged in morally serious debate claim their authority from the same criteria and incoherent when cast in the language it claims to undermine. This is to say not that we can stipulate the universal standards of historical truth but that we can identify the specific standards that are assumed to legitimate a given claim.

The decision about whether, and according to what criteria, to tell the truth about the remote or recent past is a moral choice. To distinguish incompatible criteria of historical truth is to clarify that choice.

Chapter 1

For truth, instead of being a bourgeois virtue, is the mainspring

of all human progress.—John Dewey

John Dewey, the "Trial" of Leon Trotsky, and the Search for Historical Truth

Consider the following historical text:

In 1937, new facts came to light regarding the fiendish crimes of the Bukharin-Trotsky gang. The trial of Pyatakov, Radek and others, the trial of Tukhachevsky, Yakir and others, and, lastly, the trial of Bukharin, Rykov, Rosengoltz and others, all showed that the Bukharinites and Trotskyites had long ago joined to form a common band of enemies of the people, operating as the "Bloc of Rights and Trotskyites."

The trials showed that these dregs of humanity, in conjunction with the enemies of the people, Trotsky, Zinoviev and Kamenev, had been in conspiracy against Lenin, the Party and the Soviet state ever since the early days of the October Socialist Revolution. The insidious attempts to thwart the Peace of Brest-Litovsk at the beginning of 1918, the plot against Lenin and the conspiracy with the "Left" Socialist-Revolutionaries for the arrest and murder of Lenin, Stalin and Sverdlov in the spring of 1918, the villainous shot that wounded Lenin in the summer of 1918, the revolt of the "Left" Socialist-Revolutionaries in the summer of 1918, the deliberate aggravation of differences in the Party in 1921 with the object of undermining and overthrowing Lenin's leadership from within, the attempts to overthrow the Party leadership during Lenin's illness and after his death, the betrayal of state secrets and the supply of information of an espionage character to foreign espionage services, the vile assassination of Kirov, the acts of wrecking, diversion and explosions, the dastardly murder of Menzhinsky, Kuibyshev and Gorky—all these and similar villainies over a period of twenty years were committed, it transpired, with the participation or under the direction of Trotsky, Zinoviev, Kamenev, Bukharin, Rykov and their henchmen, at the behest of espionage services of bourgeois states.

The trials brought to light the fact that the Trotsky-Bukharin fiends, in obedience to the wishes of their masters—the espionage services of foreign states—had set out to destroy the Party and the Soviet state, to undermine the defensive power of the country, to assist foreign military intervention, to prepare the way for the defeat of the Red Army, to bring about the dismemberment of the U.S.S.R., to hand over the Soviet Maritime Region to the Japanese, Soviet Byelorussia to the Poles, and the Soviet Ukraine to the Germans, to destroy the gains of the workers and collective farmers, and to restore capitalist slavery in the U.S.S.R.

These Whiteguard pygmies, whose strength was no more than that of a gnat, apparently flattered themselves that they were the masters of the country, and imagined that it was really in their power to sell or give away the Ukraine, Byelorussia and the Maritime Region.

These Whiteguard insects forgot that the real masters of the Soviet country were the Soviet people, and that the Rykovs, Bukharins, Zinovievs and Kamenevs were only temporary employees of the state, which could at any moment sweep them out from its offices as so much useless rubbish.

These contemptible lackeys of the fascists forgot that the Soviet people had only to move a finger, and not a trace of them would be left. The Soviet court sentenced the Bukharin-Trotsky fiends to be shot.

The People's Commissariat of Internal Affairs carried out the sentence.

The Soviet people approved the annihilation of the Bukharin-Trotsky gang and passed on to next business.[1]

What should we make of this passage? Today, many readers would simply say with Pierre Vidal-Naquet that "the history of the communist party of the Soviet Union that appeared under Stalin is a lasting monument of the most murderous historical lies." But as historians we might not wish to leave it at that. What seems self-evident now was the object of bitter debate and agonizing uncertainty then. The Stalinist version of the great purges of the 1930s was not only affirmed as revealed truth but glossed, as Vidal-Naquet observes, by "liberal, apparently scholarly versions of Stalinist history" ornamented by numerous references and bibliographical notes.[2] The trials were authenticated for world opinion by appeals to the "facts" established by inference from the evidence provided in great part by the confessions of the accused.

This chapter will examine one of the most influential challenges to the authenticity of the trials, presented in public hearings before a Preliminary Commission of Inquiry headed by John Dewey (henceforth referred to as the commission or the Dewey Commission). The commission was the subcommittee of a body organized to allow Leon Trotsky—condemned in absentia as the soul of the conspiracy to overthrow the Soviet state—to present his side of the case. In effect, the Dewey Commission presided over something like a mock trial of Trotsky that simultaneously placed the entire system of Soviet political justice in the dock.[3]

The debate over the validity of the trials was a debate over the nature of the Soviet experiment, and one, as James T. Farrell and many others saw it, that posed stark, categorical alternatives. "At the time," Farrell wrote, "I, as well as others, posed this question: if the official version of the trials were true, then the co-workers of Lenin and the leaders of the Bolshevik Revolution must be considered as one of the worst gang of scoundrels in history; if the trials were a frameup then the leaders of Soviet Russia were perpetuating one of the most monstrous frameups in all history."[4] This either/or had special poignancy for those thousands throughout the world, located on the political Left, whose attitude toward the Soviet regime was crucial to their political and moral self-definition.

Poignancy of a different sort might inform our own reading of those Stalinist texts in the light of the historical skepticism that leaves us and Vidal-Naquet with the question, On what grounds might we refute "murderous historical lies?" The question of how to distinguish historical truth from falsehood was starkly posed in the irreconcilable interpretations of the purge trials, which tore apart the political Left in the 1930s. In the Soviet version, the "facts" of the case were authenticated by the deadly authority of Stalinist discourse. No one who fell within the orbit of the Soviet regime in those years needed a Foucault to remind them of the integral relationship between "knowledge" and power.

The language of Marxo-Stalinism had its peculiar structure and its linguistic figures—its tropes, modes, and emplotments, or, in Hayden White's words, its own "strategies of explanation . . . with an ideological implication that is unique to it." We might then simply stand on White's "moral and aesthetic" grounds for preferring alternative versions of the past and choose to reject this one. We suspect, however, that White would not wish to insert such a text under his rubric of "mutually exclusive, though *equally legitimate*, interpretations of the same set of historical events or the same segment of the historical process" (my emphasis).[5] That was scarcely how contemporaries in any camp would have disposed of it then.

There were some who did simply reject the Stalinist version on what Richard Rorty might now identify as ethnocentric grounds. Their intellectual solidarity—to use another Rortyan term—entailed the conviction that Stalinist discourse was integrally false.[6] Few, however, would have argued, like Rorty, that "people think that intellectuals have to give a reason why these dictators [Hitler and Stalin] were wrong. This seems to me to be a ludicrous hope."[7] It seemed very important then, especially to those aligned in the socialist and democratic camps, to know whether and wherein Stalin was right or wrong, and this was important not only in the abstract but also with reference to specific issues of great political and moral significance. One could not simply assume that Stalinists lied about or were wrong about everything and that their liberal and social-democratic antagonists were correct. I am one of those who believe that representatives of liberal and democratic regimes such as Anthony Eden and Léon Blum, who defended the noninterventionist policy in the Spanish Civil War, were wrong and that the Soviet apparatchiks, apologists, and international fellow travelers who called that policy a farce were right.

While there were a great many people whose minds were made up about the validity of the Moscow Purge Trials prior to the examination of evidence, there were many who were convinced in the light of what they perceived as evidence, and others who waited to be convinced. Ambassador Davies, whose duty was to report to Washington the truth about the trials, became convinced of their authenticity; John Dewey, who agreed to head a commission of inquiry into the case of Leon Trotsky, would conclude that the trials were a cynical travesty.

I do not intend to retell the fascinating story of the mock trial of Leon Trotsky convened in Mexico City in April 1937 by the commission chaired by John Dewey, or to beat Stalinism with an old stick, but to examine the arguments through which contemporaries justified their conclusions about the truth of contradictory histories of a recent past. The Dewey Commission was not convened to write history, and the recent past it examined was remembered as well as recorded, but issues raised with regard to the grounds for the justification of historical propositions are as applicable to the commission's conclusions as to any historical text.

In March 1936 an American section of an international committee for the defense of Leon Trotsky was organized to allow Trotsky to answer the accusations leveled against him at the Moscow trials. The question of Trotsky's guilt or innocence was practically and symbolically central not only to an evaluation of the purge trials but also to the reading of the history of Russia since 1917— practically because if the charges brought against Trotsky were false, the entire structure based on the confessions of the accused, which assigned Trotsky a central role, would disintegrate; symbolically because Leon Trotsky had become the great protagonist of a modern political Paradise Lost, expelled from the workers' paradise but still "going to and fro on the earth and walking up and down on it."

As the Preliminary Commission of Inquiry had been organized by the Committee for the Defense of Leon Trotsky, it was predictably dismissed as a tool of the "Trotskyites." This view did not plausibly dispose of John Dewey, who was certainly not a Trotskyist, who refuted Trotsky on various occasions, and who, in his seventy-eighth year, was venerated as an icon of liberal rectitude. He could, of course, be dismissed as deluded or, even better, senile; but it would be difficult to argue the latter, given the publication in 1938 of *Logic, The Theory of Inquiry*, Dewey's magnum opus in technical philosophy.

The organization and procedures of the hearings in Mexico City would be vulnerable to the criticism of those who opposed the commission's conclusions. The commission disclaimed any pretense at conducting a trial; it was to function "solely as an investigating body" to decide whether "Mr. Trotsky had a case warranting further investigations."[8] As its critics would emphasize, however, the commissioners functioned as something like magistrates and jurors, setting the ground rules, posing questions, and drawing conclusions.

The commission had four members in addition to Dewey: Benjamin Stolberg, a journalist with labor connections and a qualified admirer of Trotsky; Susan La Follette, niece of Senator Robert La Follette, writer for *The Nation*, and art critic; Otto Ruehle, a German Marxist emigré with distinguished socialist credentials; and Carleton Beals, a left-wing journalist and widely read author of books on Latin America.[9] His abrupt resignation from the commission, and condemnation of its procedures, would supply powerful ammunition to its detractors.

Trotsky was "represented" by a labor lawyer, Albert Goldman, as if in a conventional adversarial procedure, but the commission's attorney, John Finerty, did not play the role of a prosecuting attorney so much as that of a European examining magistrate orchestrating a search for the truth. This too would be a target. The arguments over procedure certainly did bear on evaluations of the commission's conclusions, but ultimately the burden of conviction would be borne by the arguments over the substance of the hearings.

There were three sorts of arguments brought to bear on the results of the investigation in Mexico City which I shall label, at some risk of parody, pragmatic, hermeneutic, and epistemological. By pragmatic arguments I intend those that spoke to the possible consequences of the trial, and therefore "what was good in the way of belief" to those somewhere on the political Left; by hermeneutic I refer to interpretations of the meaning of the trials and the commission's hearings in the larger historical context, and with reference to the values and perspective of the interpreter; and by epistemological I mean the treatment of the evidence regarding what allegedly occurred.

A prologue to the pragmatic argument over the findings of the Dewey Commission appeared two months before the inquiry in Mexico City in an "open letter to American liberals" published in the *Daily Worker* and printed a month later in *Soviet Russia Today*. This manifesto, signed by many distinguished figures on the American Left, was intended to warn American liberals against the machinations of the American Committee for the Defense of Leon Trotsky, notably its organization of an investigation of the Moscow trials. It pointed out "the real nature" of the committee as a Trotskyist front and therefore an ally of fascist and reactionary enemies of the Soviet Union, which "should be left to protect itself against treasonable plots as it saw fit." The open letter concluded:

> We ask you [The American liberals] to clarify these points, not merely because we believe that the Soviet Union needs the support of liberals at this moment when the forces of fascism, led by Hitler, threaten to engulf Europe. We believe that it is important for the progressive forces in this country that you make your position clear. The reactionary sections of the press and public are precisely the ones to seize most eagerly on the anti-Soviet attacks of Trotsky and his followers to further their own aims. We feel sure that you do not wish to be counted an ally of these forces.[10]

The argument about consequences was, of course, a principal line of the communist and fellow-traveling press, but it also weighed heavily in the balance of all those whose primary concern was the inexorable advance of fascist power. Even for those who knew the trials were wrong, Alfred Kazin recalls, "the issue was not so simple. . . . The danger was Hitler, Mussolini, Franco. . . . Although I had been revolted and disgusted by still more Moscow trials[,] . . . Fascism was still the major threat to peace."[11]

According to the editors of the *New Republic*, to open the question in the manner of the Dewey Commission would simply add to the confusion over the trials. "Meanwhile, there are more important questions than Trotsky's guilt"—among them, "the question of whether American liberals and progressives are going to work toward the end they have in common, or whether they are going to dissipate their influence by quarrels among themselves over questions that concern them at second hand."[12]

When Malcolm Cowley, influential editor and literary critic of the *New Republic*, set down his reminiscences—"without apologies or recriminations," as he puts it—of the political line he followed in the 1930s, he drew a distinction between two "factions" on the Left. One group was essentially anti-Stalinist and the other anti-Hitlerite. The latter, Cowley recalls, was primarily concerned with promoting the anti-Nazi alliance which included the Communists. Whatever one thought of Stalin's brutality, vindictiveness, and so forth, "the only sound policy was to check Hitler by any possible means and with the greatest number of allies, including Beelzebub." That wasn't precisely how Cowley had characterized Stalin at the time. In comparing the great Bolshevik antagonists in the April 7, 1937, issue of the *New Republic*, Cowley wrote, "it is now a question of war and peace and the world our children are going to live in. Stalin with all his faults and virtues represents the Communist revolution. Trotsky has come to represent the 'second revolution' that is trying to weaken it in the face of attacks from the fascist powers."[13]

Like many other liberals whose primary loyalty was to a viable Popular Front, Cowley was concerned not only with the practical political consequences of one's reading of the purge trials and therefore of the Soviet system but also with its meaning—its implications for the intelligibility of the political universe and one's relation to it. A judgment on the trials was an interpretation, a making sense of patterns of political behavior in light of each individual's moral and political location. This was an issue raised at the Mexico City hearings and elsewhere by Trotsky and his partisans, who argued that a reading of Trotsky's career and, indeed, the history of the Bolshevik revolution that granted the allegations of counterrevolutionary conspiracy and betrayal was simply unintelligible.

The Dewey Commission did give some credence to this argument, although it was also available to those antagonists who were happy to quote Trotsky against himself. In various published documents Trotsky had asserted that the Soviet bureaucracy would not relinquish power without a fight and could only be removed by "a revolutionary force." Considering this issue from a broader, "more objective," liberal perspective, some would argue that as completely consequential political actors, Trotsky and his followers had no choice but to take up any method, even alliance with fascist enemies of the Soviet Union, that might bring down the regime, which incarnated the betrayal of the workers' cause. Indeed, the regime had given them no choice, and Stalinist despotism was in effect a self-fulfilling prophecy of the treasonable activity of its proponents, who were afforded no other outlet.[14] Thus, one could both accept the essential authenticity of the trials and criticize an authoritarian regime that equated opposition to conspiracy. This was still to accept the official Soviet version of what had actually occurred.

The interpretation of the Soviet apologists was the reverse of the Trotskyists' version. The entire history of the revolution and the Soviet regime was unintelligible if the trials had been a brutal farce. For Corliss Lamont, "the Soviet regime and its achievements are indivisible; and we cannot believe that its system of justice is completely out of step with its splendid accomplishments in practically all other fields."[15] The Dewey Commission was to find this version of historical intelligibility less convincing than that of Trotsky but would ultimately base its conclusions on its understanding of what it would call "historic truth." Both the defenders of Trotsky and the Communist Party's polemicists insisted that their positions were founded on factual bedrock. And it was there that the commission intended to build its case. Evidence about past events was at the center of the hearings in Mexico City.

Since the confessions at the Moscow Trials constituted the substance of the prosecution's case against Trotsky, the Dewey Commission's investigation was to a considerable extent an evaluation of their validity. As the commission remarked, despite Vyshinsky's talk of documenting the immense conspiracy, that conspiracy had left no paper trail: none of the letters or messages, not a scrap of incriminating paper, had been preserved by the horde of inept conspirators—nothing but their word, in tailored response to the prosecutor's questions.

However, the confessions did refer to alleged events that had occurred outside the Soviet Union, and these references could be checked against publicly accessible information. This was Vyshinsky's great blunder, fully exploited by

Trotsky in Mexico City, and the decisive contribution to the conclusions of the commission.

The entire case against Trotsky at the second purge trial was predicated on the confessions of Radek and Pyatakov that they had followed Trotsky's orders in orchestrating the campaign of sabotage and political terror in the Soviet Union. These orders had to have been received abroad from Trotsky or his agents—specifically, on three major occasions that were crucial for the prosecution's scenario and became the targets of Trotsky's defense. According to the confessions, (1) several defendants met Trotsky and his son L. L. Sedov in Copenhagen in 1932 to receive seditious instructions; (2) Vladimir Romm, a former correspondent for *Izvestia*, had met Trotsky and received instructions from him in the Bois de Boulogne in July 1933; and (3) G. L. Pyatakov, a former supporter of Trotsky and a key figure in the industrialization of the Soviet Union, the self-confessed linchpin of the entire conspiratorial machine in the Soviet Union, had flown to Oslo in December 1935 and met Trotsky outside the city.

The first of these allegations had to do with testimony at the first great purge trial by one Holtzman, a self-identified courier for the conspiracy. Holtzman described a trip to Copenhagen where he had put up at a Hotel Bristol and met Trotsky's son, who took him to see his father. Holtzman's confession was implausible on various counts—notably the considerable (if not absolutely conclusive) evidence that Trotsky's son Sedov could not have been in Copenhagen on that date. But the really embarrassing gaffe lay in the fact that the only Hotel Bristol in Copenhagen had been destroyed by a fire in 1917. The answer to this would be a photograph—published, among other places, in *Soviet Russia Today*[16]—which showed that there was an establishment described as the Café Bristol near a hotel, purporting to demonstrate that the witness had simply confused the café with the hotel. This line was shredded by Trotsky in his peroration in Mexico City: the shop was not a café but a candy store; it was not next to the hotel but two doors away, and it faced on another street. Holtzman had testified that he had put up at the hotel and met Sedov in the lobby. A glance at the photograph, which blacked out an area between the candy store and the hotel, carries considerable negative authority.

Vladimir Romm, who described himself as the link between Trotsky and the old Bolshevik leader Radek, testified to a meeting in the Bois de Boulogne during Trotsky's sojourn in France in 1933. The Trotsky defense presented many witnesses to the chronology of Trotsky's journey from the Mediterranean village of Cassis, where he entered France, to his French residence at Royan, where he arrived on July 25, and to the state of his health, which made it impossible for him to travel for the rest of the summer. The answer to this, of course, would be to claim that every relevant witness had lied.

The most important and contestable matter of fact would be contained in Pyatakov's testimony, which was the keystone of the entire structure erected by Vyshinsky at the second purge trial and was really indispensable for the plausibility of all three of the great trials. Pyatakov had confessed that he had been in Berlin in December 1935 on Soviet business, had flown with a forged passport to an aerodrome in Oslo and driven to Trotsky's residence, where he received instructions and learned that Trotsky was working with the Nazis. Before the trial had even concluded, Norwegian newspapers uncovered the fact that no foreign aircraft had landed at Oslo's airport during the month of December 1935 and that no foreign plane at all had used the field between September 1935 and May 1936. This rather remarkable discrepancy was assigned decisive weight in the Dewey Commission's conclusions because the entire edifice of "contradictions and deliberate falsifications" that had been erected by the prosecution depended on Pyatakov's testimony.[17]

The evidence about matters of fact constituted the basis for the commission's findings in its report *Not Guilty*, published at the end of the year. The commission assayed the credibility of the trials in the larger context of the shoddy legal procedures, the absence of relevant documentation, the perspective of Trotsky's life and writings, and the implausibility of the entire conspiratorial scenario; but the basis of its conclusions rested on the evidence that the key confessions involved factual fabrications.

In effect, the commission applied canons of evidence appropriate to both historical and legal investigations. Especially relevant were those characterized in Nicholas Rescher and Carey B. Joynt's article "Evidence in History and in the Law"[18] as the Argument from Silence and the Best Evidence Rule, and the Critical Use of Witness Testimony. The first rule proceeds from the assumption that when the best evidence relevant to the case is not produced by the party that controls it, "the law draws the inference that it would be unfavorable" to that party. Vyshinsky's crew sedulously avoided the pursuit of evidence that would have undermined the credibility of the confessions, such as the official records of the flight to Norway. As to the evaluation of witness testimony, the decisive criterion would be "the physical improbability of the facts related," and that criterion was, and remains, central to any judgment of historical truth in the case of Leon Trotsky.

It is, of course, much easier to assay the weight of the evidence now than it was then. The mutually corroborating confessions carried considerable authority. This sort of evidence is given due weight by juries and historians. But the evidence about "physical improbability" takes priority. A "cast-iron alibi" such as the absence of the accused from the scene of the crime carries an authority rarely outweighed by other evidence.

The contemporary responses to the commission's report, to Dewey's speeches setting out its conclusions, and to the entire procedure in Mexico City were more or less predictable in the light of political *partis pris*. From the beginning the hearings had seemed a dubious enterprise, not only to hard-line Stalinists and consistent fellow travelers but also to many "open-minded" liberals and independent radicals.[19] Once underway they were denigrated by ad hominem slander and coarse vituperation but also by clever argument. Consider, for example, the masterful application of selective skepticism by the journalists sent down to Mexico City by the *New Masses* to observe the hearings.[20]

Their obvious task was to disparage the entire procedure—to present it as a travesty of a trial, in which the Trotskyite "court" had stacked all of the cards in favor of the defendant. They were provided with powerful ammunition by the resignation of a member of the commission. Carleton Beals, who had been the only hostile interrogator of Trotsky, quarreled with the other members, resigned before the end of the hearings, and issued a widely published statement that described them as a whitewash: "The hushed adoration of the other members of the Commission for Mr. Trotsky throughout the hearings has defeated all spirit of honest investigation."[21]

Beals's motives are still subject to debate. He has been described as a Stalinist plant. His indignant denials of bias, publicly and in private correspondence, have been accepted by his biographer. In my view they are not convincing.[22]

The two reporters for the *New Masses* addressed not just the form of the hearings but also their substance, outlining an analysis of Trotsky's defense under two rubrics: "argument from personality, devoted to showing that it was morally and psychologically impossible for him to have engaged in treasonable counterrevolutionary activities," and "argument from 'actual facts' designed to show by circumstance and 'documentation' that Trotsky had not met or conspired with Moscow trial defendants."[23] The *New Masses* handled the first category by referring to those writings by Trotsky which asserted that the Soviet bureaucracy could be overthrown only by a new political revolution and that opposition to the will of the Soviet masses would be answered with violence.

What is more interesting for our purposes is the deft disposal of the key factual allegations. The treatment of the visit to Copenhagen emphasized the reliance on the unsupported word of Trotsky, his son, and his friends; cited Beals's questions designed to raise the possibility that Sedov could have entered Denmark with a false passport; and played on the location of a Café Bristol as featured in the photo published in *Soviet Russia Today*. The writers disposed of the issue of the meeting in the Bois de Boulogne by remarking that all of the supporting testimony came from Trotsky's friends and disciples, that the French government had made public no documentation of Trotsky's movements, and that therefore "the inquiry commission would simply have to take his own word for it." This was also the way they handled the Pyatakov trip to Norway. As the statement regarding the absence of foreign flights to the Oslo airport between September 1935 and May 1936 was never confirmed by the Norwegian government, "again you had to take Trotsky's word for it."[24]

Readers of the *New Masses* might have believed in its writers' objectivity; they scarcely expected impartiality. But there were plenty of ostensibly impartial observers who arrived at the same conclusions as the *New Masses* or *Soviet Russia Today*. Walter Duranty in the *New York Times* and Joseph Barnes of the *Herald-Tribune* underwrote the validity of the purge trials. The *New Republic* published Duranty's "Riddle of Russia," where he simply summarized the Soviet line on the crimes of the Trotsky center, qualified by the familiar observation that opponents in the Soviet state had no choice but to work underground, therefore to conspire, therefore to commit treason.[25]

For many liberals and social democrats who stood somewhere between consistent fellow travelers and the anticommunist Left, the polemical cacophony over the trials induced something like logical anomie. At various times in 1937 and even after the third purge trial, in 1938, the editors of the *New Republic* and the *Nation* assumed a position of "Agnosticism on the Moscow Trials"—the title of a *New Republic* editorial. Perhaps the confessions were not completely convincing, they argued, but as it was impossible for foreigners fully to explore the evidence on either side, the fairest position was to suspend judgment.[26] As Frank Warren observed in his book *Liberals and Communism*,[27] the agnostic position and the argument that American intellectuals should suspend judgment to preserve unity in the Left effectively supported the Soviet status quo.

I don't intend to examine the various motives of the liberal intellectuals who more or less swallowed the party line (a subject thoughtfully treated in Warren's book), except with regard to the way that evidence about Trotsky's guilt or innocence was assimilated, refuted, or explained away. Nor do I wish to score points off my deluded predecessors with the complacency of facile hindsight, or to suggest that a qualified defense of historical objectivity is an affirmation of political conservatism.

By April 1937, the agnostic position had been superseded, to the satisfaction of Malcolm Cowley and many others, by the conviction that "the major part of the indictment was proved without much possibility of doubting it." Cowley did grant that some points depending on the testimony on Pyatakov's flight to Oslo seemed less firmly established. "On these points," he wrote, "we might suspend our judgment until more conclusive evidence is produced by one side or the other. The main question to be decided here is the scrupulousness and good faith of the Soviet authorities. It does not seem to me that Trotsky's moral guilt or innocence is really at stake."[28]

This remarkable approach was restated by the editors of the journal in response to the publication of the Dewey Commission report (which they hadn't "fully read"). The fact of Leon Trotsky's guilt or innocence did not answer the question of whether there was a conspiracy or speak to its obvious repercussions on international politics and the peace of the world. "Americans were more concerned with that than with allegations that Trotsky was its master mind."[29]

That chord was struck again by F. L. Schuman in a full-scale treatment of the case in the *Southern Review*, which reads something like "The Fellow Traveler's Guide to the Trials."[30] Having described himself as a political scientist and a liberal who "abjures both Stalinism and Trotskyism and abhors dictatorship and terrorism in all their forms," Schuman summarized the contradictory interpretations of the Trials, stated that there was insufficient evidence for an outside observer, such as the Dewey Commission, to arrive at a definitive judgment, and then did arrive, concluding that "the available testimony points unmistakably to the guilt of the accused and to the sincerity and substantial accuracy of the confessions."[31]

Schuman managed to ring changes in the various pragmatic, hermeneutic, and epistemological arguments that affirmed the truth of the trials. Thus along with reflections on the political meaning of Trotsky's role as the fallen angel of the revolution, and the worldwide consequences of opposition to the practical, consequential, antifascist leadership of the Soviet regime, Schuman confronted the evidence about actual events produced by the Trotsky defense before the Dewey Commission. In considering the three crucial allegations of the Trotsky defense—no meeting in Copenhagen, no rendezvous at the Bois de Boulogne, no Pyatakov journey to the empty airfield in Oslo—Schuman pleaded the absence of any verifiable testimony. As for Copenhagen, there were only the denials of Trotsky and his son and the testimony of their friends (Schuman did grant in passing that Moscow's photographic evidence on the Café Bristol is not quite convincing); as for the Paris rendezvous, "it is Trotsky's word against Romm's with no conclusive evidence from the French authorities available"; as for Pyatakov's flight, he "travelled incognito and his plane may have landed in some obscure spot without being officially noticed." Trotsky had been caught in politically expedient falsehoods in the past, Schuman continued, so there was no reason to suppose that his unsupported testimony outweighed the mutually supporting confessions at the trials.

On top of all of this Schuman took out a little polemical insurance: "Even should all the allegations be disproved, Trotsky must remain under suspicion of complicity until he has demonstrated convincingly that he proposed to remove Stalin and to organize revolution against 'the bureaucracy' by methods other than those he was said to have employed."[32]

In subsequent issues, the *Southern Review* featured correspondence for and against Schuman's essay that followed the factional fault line on the American Left.[33] In a characteristic, ferociously cogent article, Sidney Hook concentrated his fire on Schuman's attempt to explain away the evidence regarding matters of fact presented before the commission in Mexico City.[34] Here, as throughout the debate on the trials, Hook hammered away at the factual question. "Guilt on all the matters charged," he wrote, "is a matter of evidence."[35]

This was Dewey's emphasis, too, as he presented and defended the conclusions of the Preliminary Commission of Inquiry. In a speech that he delivered after the deliberations of the commission but before publication of its final report, Dewey remarked that many honest liberals seemed to assume Trotsky's guilt because they believed that his theories and policies were mistaken. Here they suffered from the "intellectual and moral confusion that is the great weakness of professed liberals, for Trotsky was not convicted upon charges of theoretical and political opposition to the regime which exists in the Soviet Union. He was convicted upon certain definite charges whose truth or falsity is a matter of objective fact." The Dewey Commission was "trying to get at the truth as to the specific charges upon which he was convicted. This work is one of evidence and objective fact, not of weighing theories against each other."[36]

In his refutations of the commission's critics, Dewey seems to grant a hard autonomy to the "objective facts." Whether this approach is compatible with his instrumentalist version of inquiry and his conviction that "truth-falsity is not a property of propositions,"[37] or can be reconciled with Richard Rorty's celebration of "Dewey's suspicion of attempts to contrast an objective 'given' (e.g., 'the evidence,' 'the facts') with human 'takings,' "[38] I leave to those who are better equipped than I to say.

In the brief section on historical inquiry in Dewey's *Logic* there are passages that seem to promise small comfort to the historical objectivist. Dewey argues that the notion that historical inquiry simply reinstates the events that once happened "as they actually happened" is incurably naive, that "all historical construction is necessarily selective [and] necessarily written from the stand-point of the present [and] of that which is contemporaneously judged to be important in the present," and that "the writing of history is itself an historical event—it has existential consequences. . . . [T]here is no history except in terms of movement toward some outcome[;] . . . history cannot escape its own process. It will, therefore, always be rewritten."[39]

On the other hand, in the same section of the book Dewey refers to the control that must be exercised "with respect to the authenticity of evidential data" and grants that "it is certainly legitimate to say that a certain thing happened in a certain way at a certain time in the past, in case adequate data have been procured and critically handled." Dewey then qualifies this conces-sion to an objectively discernible past: "But the statement, 'it actually hap-pened in this way' has its status and significance *within* the scope and per-spective of historical writing. It does not determine the logical conditions of historical propositions, much less the identity of these propositions with events in their original occurrence."[40]

Even with this qualifier, it is the assumption that statements about the past can be categorically true or false that allows the Dewey Commission to state "in the most categorical fashion that on the basis of all the evidence we find them [the accused at the purge trials] not guilty of having conspired with Leon Trotsky and Leon Sedov for any purpose whatsoever."[41]

Presumably, the commission and Dewey himself had answered to their satisfaction Dewey's question, which in my view is the question to put to all claims of historical truth: "What conditions must be satisfied in order that there may be grounded propositions regarding a sequential course of past events? The question is not even whether judgments about remote events can be made with *complete* warrant much less is it whether 'History can be a science.' It is: upon what grounds are some judgments about a course of past events more entitled to credence than certain other ones?"[42]

Dewey's "upon what grounds" is not equivalent to "according to what facts." Past events are not immediate; they are inferred. The authentication of Pyatakov's testimony depended not on immediately perceptible events but on inference from evidence. The point at which conflicting histories become incommensurable is not in contradictory versions of what actually happened but in fundamentally different criteria for establishing the truth.

The criteria for establishing the truth—the norms of valid inference— affirmed by the Dewey Commission and by the Soviet court were ostensibly identical but actually incommensurable. This was because the grounds for Stalinist belief were located in the party line. The Leninist argument that conceptions of truth were relative to social class, but that the class truths of the proletariat were congruent with reality, had been streamlined into a sort of Stalinist Thomism where the faithful had only to reaffirm by Reason the articles of faith bestowed by Revelation. Or, to borrow David Joravsky's characterization, Soviet ideology did not distinguish "between service of group interests and objective verification as essentially different bases for belief."[43]

What I wish to emphasize with regard to the international debate over the purge trials is that this essential criterion could not be acknowledged by the apologists for the Soviet line. That is, however sincerely they believed in the inerrancy of the Soviet leadership, or however cynically they lied in the light of that assumption, they could not simply assert it as their sole claim to authority. Their polemics did not afford the clarity about conflicting criteria for truth that one can see, for example, in those fundamentalists who assert the inerrancy of Scripture irrespective of any sort of evidence bearing the authority of science or common sense. In principle, this is where the argument ends. In fact, even creationists whose ultimate authority is a certain reading of biblical text are glad to cite "scientific" refutations of carbon dating. When it is polemically convenient, they too claim the cognitive authority of science and common sense. So did Stalin.[44]

For communist polemicists circa 1937 there could be no question about the objective validity of the findings of Soviet courts. The confessions alone were sufficient to establish the truth beyond any reasonable doubt. However, like a tongue to a sore tooth, party-line apologists kept returning to the manifest discrepancies between the confessions and the evidence regarding relevant time and place outside Russia. Even before the end of the Pyatakov trial Vyshinsky was impelled by the reports of the absence of flights to the Oslo airport to put "in the records" the following communication: "The consular department of the People's Commissariat of Foreign Affairs hereby informs the Procurator of the U.S.S.R. that according to information received by the embassy of the U.S.S.R. in Norway the Kjellere Aerodrome near Oslo receives all the year round, in accordance with international regulations, airplanes of other countries, and that the arrival and departure of airplanes is possible also in the winter months."[45] This feeble attempt to shore up the system of interdependent fabrications at its weakest point was followed some months later by the circulation of the "Café" Bristol photograph intended to validate the testimony on the Copenhagen connection.

William Z. Foster's *Questions and Answers on the Piatakov-Radek Trial* is a fair example of the many made-to-order polemics against the critics of the trials.[46] Foster did a rather good job of steering away from the evidential issues. He dismissed the absence of supporting documentation as the obvious result of the practical imperatives of conspiring, and he persuasively argued the implausibility of scripting and staging the complex scenario required by the trials, applying Ockham's razor, as it were, to Trotsky's throat. This argument seemed plausible to many reasonably open-minded liberals, as it appealed to the sense of how things worked in general without requiring the consideration of the credibility of specific claims. However, Foster felt obliged to dispose of the hard factual issues in passing: he straightened out the question of the location of the Café Bristol and dismissed "other Trotsky attacks upon the Oslo airplane incident, the Russian visit to Trotsky, etc." as based on "similar quibbles."

A more subtle response to the embarrassing factual discrepancies in the confessions was suggested by Joshua Kunitz in the *New Masses*. Kunitz surmised that some of the accused had made absurd confessions describing events that could not have occurred in order to discredit Soviet justice.[47] This line worked to defuse the critique of the obvious flaws in the confessions by vaguely granting their existence without drawing the specific consequences for the credibility of the entire indictment.

These examples of party-line polemic illustrate the fact that the Stalinists and the Dewey Commission ostensibly spoke the same language—that is, appealed to the same criteria of historical judgment in the case of Leon Trotsky. According to Soviet spokesmen it was perfectly clear that the facts of the case imposed the conclusion of the courts. For Dewey, Hook, and other critics of the Trials, as the confessions were demonstrably false, the entire case collapsed.

For the worldwide agglomeration of dedicated antifascists, fellow travelers, left-leaning liberals, and independent socialists who did not, or believed they did not, receive the party line as if from Sinai, things were not so simple. They too accepted the rules of rational discourse and "objective" investigation yet wished to evade their unwelcome conclusions. That is why some of them arrived at the phenomenally incoherent thesis of the irrelevance of the issue of Trotsky's guilt or innocence—a formulation as unacceptable to hard-line party liners as to anti-Stalinist logicians.

The thesis of the irrelevance of Trotsky's guilt or innocence was raised to a higher level of abstraction in arguments that attempted to substitute the authority of ultimate meaning for that of plausible inference. In this version the highest court of appeal was a hypostatized History whose judgment was validated not by an understanding of the past but by a reading of the future. If argued with excessive clarity, this approach simply reads as vulgar pragmatism—"The winners write the history"; but given the appropriate transcendental twist, it lifts the conversation above the question of mere fact into a higher realm. This sort of argument was only brought to full continental flower after the war, by Maurice Merleau-Ponty.[48]

A rather inchoate contemporary historicist interpretation of the trials was advanced in the *Workers' Age*, organ of the Lovestoneites, the American partisans of Bukharin. The issue of February 13, 1937, drew an analogy between the purge trials and the political trials of the French Revolution, remarking that it was pointless to pass judgment on the validity of the condemnations of the Girondists and the other victims of Jacobin justice. "In effect, we practically ignore the charges, refutations and counter-charges, and ask ourselves: which tendency was carrying forward the interests of the revolution, and which was obstructing it?" Projecting this criterion into the twentieth century, an "objective judgment" on the Moscow Trials proceeded from the view that "the course of events has generally confirmed the viewpoint of Stalin as against that of Trotsky on the vital questions of socialist construction in the Soviet

Union, on the tempo of industrialization and on the collectivization of agriculture." This interpretation coincided with the conviction that there was indeed a "substantial bedrock of fact" supporting the accusations against the followers, or former followers, of Trotsky and Zinoviev.[49]

As the "course of events" came to include more trials and other victims, the Lovestoneites began to reexamine the grounds for judging Soviet justice. By the time the handwriting on the wall spelled Bukharin, Will Herberg and Bertram Wolfe had been convinced by the Dewey Commission report that the crucial admissions of Holtzman, Romm, and Pyatakov were a tissue of falsehoods constituting a "brazen . . . political frame up." The trials were still best understood from a "historico-political rather than a juridical point of view," but from that viewpoint it was apparent that the trials were actually a phenomenon of Stalin's desperate attempt to preserve an oppressive, reactionary regime.

A more sophisticated attempt to transform a vulgar argument from consequences into an interpretation of the trials' essential meaning (without completely avoiding the question of consequences) was Merleau-Ponty's critique of Koestler's *Darkness at Noon*. In a series of articles in *Les Temps Modernes* in 1946 and 1947, collected in his book *Humanism and Terror*, Merleau-Ponty staked out grounds for judgment that were, I would argue, incommensurable with those asserted by Dewey *or* his procommunist antagonists in the 1930s.

Merleau-Ponty located the authority for interpreting past events in a possible reading of the future, such that a record of what Dewey had called the objective facts was not the decisive consideration for the evaluation of the trials. While he recognized the extreme implausibility of Vyshinsky's scenario—he remarked that "it would truly be strange if Lenin had surrounded himself with supporters all of whom except one were capable of crossing over into the service of capitalist governments"[50]—he dismissed such criticisms as inessential.

To some extent Merleau-Ponty did accept the argument from consequences. He interpreted Bukharin's testimony in the third trial as an admission by Bukharin himself of the treasonable implications of what might have been a perfectly honest and rational critique of the regime: "The Moscow Trials might be seen as the drama of subjective honesty and objective treason."[51] Under certain circumstances an interpretation based on an "enlargement and falsification of the facts . . . remains historically permissible because political man is defined not by what he himself does but by the forces on which he counts." Thus, in a political universe in which to make any choice is to do violence to others, "to tell the truth and act out of conscience are nothing but alibis of a false morality; true morality is not concerned with what we think or what we want but obliges us to take a historical view of ourselves."[52]

Yet according to Merleau-Ponty, such a historical view is always problematic, because of the radical contingency of human destinies. The question of whether the Soviet system would be the political expression of a proletariat that was to fulfill its assigned role as the universal class remained open. Therefore, the ultimate judgment of the trials rested with the tribunal of the future—a position that, as Raymond Aron observed, would logically postpone history's judgment on the trials until the Last Judgment.[53]

Although John Dewey's philosophy seems light-years away from the Marxism-existentialism of Merleau-Ponty circa 1947, Dewey too argued that the question of whether a proposition about the past is true depends on present and future events. Valid propositions about events that occurred in the past can only be based on what is presently observable, and furthermore, the history under determination extends into the future. Only when past, present, and future events are brought into "temporal continuity with each other" are propositions about past events fully warranted.[54] This is Dewey's way of approaching the historical evidence. The definition of something presently experienced as historical evidence depends on the questions posed to the past—in Dewey's terms, "the inquiry." Thus the report on the absence of flights to the Oslo airport is evidence in the context of the investigation of Pyatakov's testimony about what actually happened in the past, which itself is significant because it relates to the ongoing inquiry regarding the alleged anti-Soviet conspiracy. This process suggests further investigation, thus projecting our assessment of judgments about the past into the future. Dewey's emphasis on the temporal continuum of validation is far different from Merleau-Ponty's location of judgment in some undefined future. In Merleau-Ponty's language it does not essentially matter whether Pyatakov made that trip to Oslo; to Dewey, that is precisely what matters.

For John Dewey, the obligation to tell the truth as a necessary constituent of a democratic polity took priority over the immediate, or distant, political consequences of any particular inquiry. Such a commitment entails one of the senses in which objectivity is ordinarily defined. Dewey's objectivity in this sense is recalled in James T. Farrell's description of his response to the evidence presented to the commission: "He [Dewey] went to Mexico more or less thinking that Stalin rather than Trotsky was right. On the basis of the evidence that Trotsky presented plus what Dewey read on the Moscow Trials, he came to the conclusion that Trotsky and the other defenders were right. However, he did not agree with Trotsky's political views."[55]

If Farrell's recollections were correct, Dewey was objective in the ordinary sense of what people mean when they say that someone is disinterested. "Disinterested," however, is not the equivalent of "neutral"; it is possible to be passionately dispassionate. Or to put it in currently fashionable language, Dewey's commitment to objectivity in this sense did not transcend the "historicity" of such a commitment. The decision to tell the truth according to his lights, irrespective of the consequences, was a socially, historically, morally mediated choice—just as one might have chosen to ignore the facts and grind an axe.

Objectivity in another sense was involved in Dewey's choice of the criteria for judging the truth of propositions about the past, in his choice of "the grounds on which some judgments about a course of past events [are] more entitled to credence than certain other ones." These are the grounds that impelled Dewey to identify some arguments about Trotsky's guilt or innocence as good—for example, those which spoke to the "physical improbability of the facts related"—and others as bad—for example, those emphasizing Trotsky's personality, or the virtues of the Soviet system, or the consequences for the Popular Front.

To put it another way, the correct assertions that past events are mediated through present preconceptions, that conflicting interpretations of complex events are rarely settled by definitive demonstrations, that historical interpretations are dependent on the language in which they are cast, or that it is impossible to evaluate discrete bits of evidence outside of temporal and ideological contexts, do not justify the stance of agnosticism toward the Moscow trials that was affected by many of the 1930s liberals. It is understandable that men and women of good will took that stance; they were mistaken. The sound arguments on Pyatakov's flight now seem virtually self-evident, independent of Khrushchev's revelations or anything else we have learned since 1956. No one now accepts the bad arguments.

We now find the commission's conclusions more persuasive than those of William Z. Foster, Malcolm Cowley, or F. L. Schuman, not because of their superior tropological strategies, or because of a skillful parade of rhetorical figures, or the hermeneutic fusing of historical horizons, or a dialogic interaction between this reader and those texts, but because they satisfy familiar criteria of empirical inference and rational discourse. This is not to deny that all arguments, including Dewey's and mine, are rhetorical in some sense, but to argue that rhetorical preferences do not exempt historical discourse from evidential norms.

Perhaps one might say that all of this amounts to kicking an open door, that no sane person denies that some statements about past events are true and some are false. But that brings us back to Dewey's question: on what grounds do we prefer one historical account to another; on what grounds do we identify errors and refute lies?

According to Sidney Hook's memoirs, his answer to that question was crucially affected by the experience of the trials:

> The upshot of the Moscow trials affected my epistemology, too. I had been prepared to recognize that understanding the past was in part a function of our need to cope with the present and future, that rewriting history was in a sense a method of making it. But the realization that such a view easily led to the denial of objective historical truth, to the cynical view that not only is history written by the survivors but that historical truth is created by the survivors—which made untenable any distinction between historical fiction and truth—led me to rethink some aspects of my objective relativism. Because nothing was absolutely true and no one could know the whole truth about anything, it did not follow that it was impossible to establish any historical truth beyond a reasonable doubt. Were this to be denied, the foundations of law and society would ultimately collapse. Indeed, any statement about anything may have to be modified or withdrawn in the light of additional evidence, but only on the assumption that the additional evidence has not been manufactured. At any point in time, the upshot of converging lines of evidence must guide judgment.[56]

I am sure that there are those who would ask Hook to justify the universal standards that distinguish historical fiction from truth—to specify the location of some historical Archimedes' point. But he would not have to answer them if they justified their arguments, explicitly or implicitly, in his language. And if they spoke a completely different language there would be no dialogue. If Hook's political opponents had simply located the criterion of truth-value in Stalin's bosom there would have been no way for Hook to refute them, but they would have lost all credibility even with those who were desperate to be credulous.

Hook's decision too was a moral choice, but without that choice there are no grounds on which to refute murderous historical lies.

Chapter 2

As proofs, forged documents, in general, are better than genuine ones, first of all because they have been expressly made to suit the needs of the case, to order and measure, and therefore they are fitting and exact. They are also preferable because they carry the mind into an ideal world and turn it aside from the reality which, alas! in this world is never without some alloy. . . . Nevertheless, I think I should have preferred . . . that we had no proofs at all.

—Anatole France, *Penguin Island*

Versions of Truth in the Dreyfus Case

There are some recent pasts so politically and morally charged as to preempt any neutral accounting, when even the attempt to stand aside is to take a stand. This was the case for the contemporaries of the Dreyfus affair. Even now, the assumption of neutrality lent by distance has not guaranteed a perfect consensus. The affair remains "an inexhaustible subject for meditation." These are the words of the novelist-critic Maurice Blanchot in a sensitive, reflective essay stimulated by Jean-Denis Bredin's fine work on the affair. Blanchot's meditation concerns, among other questions, the moral necessity of the political *engagement* of the "autonomous intellectual," and its inevitable creative costs. I will meditate here on the question of truth in, or about, the affair and on what Blanchot characterizes as the inseparability of morality and rationality.[1]

While the affair does continue to provide a subject for meditation, and not only for historians, it is one of those "memorable" occasions whose memory has congealed into a few more or less accurate clichés. Probably the most common image of the affair even among fairly well informed people, in as well as out of France, is not so far from that of a student who once wrote in an exam that Dreyfus was condemned for his race, religion, and handwriting. Therefore, a brief outline and chronology might be appropriate without, I hope, insulting the intelligence of the historically literate.

In September 1894 the "Statistical Section" of the French army—that is, the intelligence service—acquired a list or schedule (in French a *bordereau*) of secrets apparently conveyed by a French officer to the German military attaché in Paris. The listed items suggested to the members of the Statistical Section that the traitor might have been a gunner attached to the General Staff. A Jewish officer who fit that description, Captain Alfred Dreyfus, was arrested, interrogated, and arraigned before a military court. The crime and the suspect's identity were leaked to certain newspapers and immediately taken up by the anti-Semitic press, which put great pressure on the authorities to bring in a conviction.

Under brutal grilling, Dreyfus refused to confess. Handwriting experts disagreed on whether samples of his writing matched that of the *bordereau*. Various fellow officers testified about his generally disagreeable character, but it was difficult to assign a plausible motive to a wealthy, ambitious officer from an Alsatian family that had chosen France after their province was seized by Germany in 1871. Faced with the possibility that Dreyfus would be acquitted, the prosecution presented a secret dossier to the court martial without submitting it to the defense. Dreyfus was convicted and was sentenced to perpetual deportation in a fortified enclosure (Devil's Island) and to military degradation.

At that time no one outside of a tight military circle was aware of the illegal submission of the secret dossier or the fact that the documents in the dossier had been doctored to strengthen the case against the accused. Therefore, aside from the captain's attorney and immediate family, no one questioned the verdict of the court.

There the case rested until March 1896, when Colonel Georges Picquart, who had recently been appointed director of the intelligence service, came upon a document apparently obtained, like the *bordereau*, from the wastebasket of the German attaché. It was a draft of a note—a letter-telegram called a *petit-bleu*—to a French officer, a Major Esterhazy. In the course of the investigation of this notoriously dissolute and debt-ridden character, Picquart chanced upon a sample of Esterhazy's writing that immediately struck him as identical with that of the *bordereau*. When he brought this to the attention of his superiors, he was told to "keep the affairs separate." As it became apparent that Picquart would refuse to bury the issue, he was posted to the military frontier in Tunisia.

By the end of 1896 the Dreyfus case resurfaced in public consciousness through leaks to the press and a remarkable pamphlet by Bernard Lazare that challenged the legality and validity of the verdict. At this point the Dreyfus case had become the sensational affair. The anxiety of the High Command and the anger of those who were eventually designated as the anti-Dreyfusards were aroused when it became known that the distinguished vice president of the Senate, C. A. Scheurer-Kestner, having been informed of Picquart's discoveries, had expressed doubts about the justice of the original verdict. The publication of a facsimile of the *bordereau* which could then be compared with the handwriting of Alfred Dreyfus and eventually with that of Esterhazy contributed significantly to the formation of a circle of "revisionists" soon to be locked in bitter public conflict with the army's defenders.

With the approval of their superiors, the members of the intelligence service responded to the growing revisionist campaign by complicated maneuvers intended to shield Esterhazy and implicate Picquart. The solution to Esterhazy's vulnerability was to bring him before a court martial that duly exonerated him. This seemed to lay the affair to rest, especially as an overwhelming majority in the Chamber of Deputies categorically repudiated any proposal to reexamine the verdict of the original court.

However, the public perception of the affair was transformed by the publication in January 1898 of Émile Zola's "J'Accuse," in which the chiefs of the military establishment were accused of responsibility for a consciously orchestrated miscarriage of justice. Zola's highly charged polemic was designed to provoke legal reprisal and a trial that might become a forum for public exposure of the machinations of the military cabal. This trial brought the simmering passions that had attended the affair to a boil. Mobs gathered outside the court and in the streets of the cities. Anti-Semitism became a popular political force, and the anger aroused by the revisionist campaign turned against the republic itself. While the majority of the republic's political elite continued to affirm Dreyfus's guilt, the anti-Dreyfusard movement clustered around the pole of traditional hostility to republican institutions reflecting the convictions of a section of the Catholic Church, the nostalgic aristocracy, the officer caste, and a new brand of ultranationalism that fused a populist demagoguery with antidemocratic goals. The intelligentsia was polarized over the affair and played an increasingly visible role in both camps. A section of the socialist and labor movement led by Jean Jaurès concluded that it should join the battle in the Chamber and in the streets, in defense of bourgeois democracy and individual rights.

Zola's trial on charges of defaming respected military officers, his conviction, and his flight to England seemed fatal to the revisionist cause. The generals called upon to testify at the trial referred with great effect to secret documents proving Dreyfus's guilt—documents whose disclosure would risk war with Germany.

At this point, the determination of the new minister of war, Godefroy Cavaignac, to provide an irrefutable public demonstration of Dreyfus's guilt blew the case open. The officer assigned to reexamine the dossier discovered that the key document mentioning Dreyfus by name was a crude forgery that, along with other fabricated or altered pieces of "evidence," had been added to the file by Colonel Henry, the central figure in the vendetta of the Statistical Section against Dreyfus and his defenders. Henry was arrested, imprisoned, and found in his cell with his throat cut—allegedly a suicide. After the exposure of these forgeries as well as other counterfeit letters mailed to Dreyfus and Picquart, the tide began to run to the Dreyfusards.

The response of the militant anti-Dreyfusards was to celebrate Henry's "patriotic forgery" and collect subscriptions to a memorial in support of the patriotic martyr's wife and children. The messages accompanying the contributions to the memorial were characterized by a ferocious anti-Semitism in words that anticipate the practices of the twentieth century.

By 1899, the accumulated evidence about the identity of the real traitor and the gradual shift in mainstream political opinion in response to the perceived threat to the existence of the republic enabled the High Appeals Court to annul the original verdict, in light of the illegal procedure, and impose a retrial—once again before a military court. This was the trial at Rennes in August and September 1899. Under immense pressure, before a deeply divided nation, the second court martial once again found Dreyfus guilty, this time with the ludicrous codicil of "extenuating circumstances."

In the same year, a new republican coalition, the so-called Waldeck-Rousseau government, which reflected the transformation of the dominant attitudes toward the affair in the Chamber of Deputies, decided to close the case by granting Dreyfus a pardon. Dreyfus and his family decided to accept the pardon, for which he was never forgiven by some of the zealots for his cause. In 1906 the Appeals Court annulled the second verdict. Dreyfus returned to the army and served as a lieutenant colonel in the First World War.

The immediate and distant consequences of the affair were not terminated by the closing of the case, but for my purposes here it is sufficient to say that truth had prevailed. While a penumbra of doubt still clings to certain salient aspects of the story—such as whether the *bordereau* had really been discovered in the office of the German attaché; the identity of the author of the *petit-bleu*; or the real relations between Henry and Esterhazy before the affair began—eventually, even in France, there came to be an authoritative consensus on the truth at the core of the Dreyfus case in a narrow sense, as distinguished from the broad interpretation of the affair. Now almost, if not quite (a rather strident not quite), everyone believes that Dreyfus was innocent. In that sense, the truth is, and was, on the side of the Dreyfusards. Truthfulness in a larger sense has often been attributed to the best of the Dreyfusard partisans with regard to their "rigorous concern for facts, the requirements of demonstration and logical proof, the very method which intellectuals had acquired and were inclined to extrapolate to other areas of consideration."[2]

This is Bredin's characterization—a descendant of the original self-image of the Dreyfusards, which has often been reproduced by their sympathizers. For example, in his book *More Than a Trial: The Struggle over Captain Dreyfus*, Robert L. Hoffman devotes most of a chapter to a distinction between the Dreyfusard scholars, "who had deliberately committed themselves to scientific rigor in their work," and those anti-Dreyfusard intellectuals who "typically were those who did not fully employ rigorous scientific methods, or did so without consciousness of and commitment to the critical rationalism that underlies that method." The Dreyfusards believed that their political purpose "would best be served by telling the truth and they were prepared to accept correction of errors they might have committed should evidence prove them wrong."[3]

While this chapter might be considered an extended commentary in support of Hoffman's interpretation, I do recognize that there are historians who would find his treatment far too simple and far too confident. Bredin himself, who has no difficulty in locating where moral right belongs, cautions against "explaining the Affair summarily as a systematic confrontation between two moralities, a clear division between men of Truth and men of Dogma."[4] While I agree with Bredin's qualifications, I will emphasize the way in which competing claims to authority in interpreting the affair came to express conflicting criteria of truth.

Others, including those with no particular French axe to grind, have gone much further than Bredin in qualifying or simply jettisoning the classic version of the affair as a conflict between liberal, humanist, rationalist Good and reactionary, racist, obscurantist Evil. Revisions of the simple celebration of the affair as the victory of the Rights of Man come in various flavors:

1. Dreyfus was and remains guilty as charged.

Certainly most of those who first heard of the affair in 1894, and for some years after that, believed that Dreyfus was guilty in the light of common sense and conventional juridical canons of truth. It has been virtually de rigueur to cite the initial response of the great Dreyfusards Jaurès and Clemenceau demanding a more severe punishment for the culprit. This conviction was supported by a rational deference to authority: a court weighed the relevant evidence and came to presumably valid conclusions, as in the normal course of events. Later, as evidence emerged that seemed to support a revision of the original decision, a sincere belief in Dreyfus's guilt was still founded on a deference to authority, partly because revisionism came to require a belief in the dishonest or at least stupid behavior of those worthy of trust and respect. After the uncovering of the forgery in the counterintelligence bureau— Colonel Henry's fabricated document—it required more ingenuity to maintain an unqualified belief in the truth of the original charge.

Then with the revelations of further fabrications, tampering with evidence, the clear implication of Esterhazy, and so forth, the strains on ingenuity increased; now what was required was a belief in the existence of esoteric proofs, such as undisclosable documents in the Kaiser's hand. Historical imagination proved equal to the task. The anti-Dreyfusard cause continues to be argued in works that claim the authority of conventional, empirical, and rational canons in order to support the original decision of the military courts.[5] Even after the publication in 1961 of the magisterial work of Marcel Thomas based on the discovery of new material in the archives,[6] anti-Dreyfusards still produce books arguing that Dreyfus was guilty in fact.[7] By this time we have arrived at a perverse appropriation of the authority of rational and empirical

discourse, of which there are even worse examples dedicated to the oblitera-
tion of twentieth-century atrocities.

*2. It doesn't matter whether or not Dreyfus was guilty; the villainy of the Dreyfusards
entailed a sort of retroactive condemnation.*

This is a variant of the argument about consequences, which I will discuss
below, but I set it off here to identify those who are not willing to agree that
Dreyfus was in fact innocent. To accept this argument is to speak the language
of Charles Maurras and Maurice Barrès. If Dreyfus were innocent, Barrès
wrote, "one thing must be refused him all the same: pardon for his defenders.
For the rest, if he is not a traitor, he should perforce be ashamed for having
aroused such sympathy."[8]

*3. Dreyfus was not guilty, but the conflict posed a genuine moral dilemma—justice at all
costs versus the health of the state.*

This is one version of what I will call the pragmatic standard, in which the
commitment to truth must be weighed in light of the consequences. If the
affair is viewed from this perspective, men of goodwill might well have taken
either position.[9] This is an approach that continues to be favored by what one
might call the British School, an early example of which is Brian Chapman's
book *The Dreyfus Case: A Reassessment.* Chapman concludes by quoting Julian
Benda, himself a committed Dreyfusard who recognized the grave political
consequences of his commitment: "the single coherent attitude for the non-
revolutionary Dreyfusist was to say either: '*I put justice before all and with death in
my soul* accept the political consequences of my act of justice'; or '*I put order above
everything else and with death in my soul* renounce an act of justice which will
inevitably bring in its train such social consequences' " (emphasis in original).[10]

A variant of this approach, and a French specialty, is to concede that Dreyfus was innocent but to conjecture that the people who framed him were
involved in a complicated game involving double agents and double-crosses
and pregnant with the threat of war—a game that could not be exposed
without blowing the intelligence network. One fairly recent example of this
theory is in the work of Henri Giscard d'Estaing, who embellishes such a
scenario with remarks on the essentially sinister behavior of the Jewish cabal in
their exploitation of this patriotic dilemma.[11] We find various sanitized versions of this approach:

4. Dreyfus was innocent, but the consequences of the affair were certainly deplorable, and the behavior of the Dreyfusard faction put them on a level with their antagonists.

This interpretation is usually accompanied by an attempt to qualify what is considered the received view of the moral alignments in which there was, as Douglas Johnson puts it, "on the one side justice, truth, and the determination to achieve them, on the other side obscurantism, prejudice, indifference, and injustice."[12] Johnson's work, often cited as the most balanced, objective account of the affair, is certainly dedicated to a reassessment of the moral balance sheet that enters all the good on the side of the Dreyfusards and various forms of evil on the other side. For Johnson, any evidence about the inherent goodwill of the generals or some understanding of their motives, even when they engaged in lies and illegality, is drawn out, and any shred of evidence about the less-than-heroic qualities even of such legendary Dreyfusard heroes as Colonel Picquart is sedulously unearthed. Having listed all of the ways in which both sides might be considered equally prejudiced, tendentious, unscrupulous, and merciless, Johnson concludes, "All this is not to say that there is no difference between anti-Dreyfusard and Dreyfusard. But it is to say that the difference between them was not one of personality, of scruples or of methods. Often, in fact, the difference was histrionic."[13]

In his book *The Fall of Public Man*, in a section entitled "The Dreyfus Affair: Destructive Gemeinschaft," Richard Sennett follows Johnson's general interpretation but locates the meaning of the affair in the essential histrionic *identity* of the two camps. Sennett provides a close reading of Zola's *J'Accuse* (and the complete text in an appendix) to show that "devoid of logical and legal substance, its purpose, would cast the affair as a drama of personal morality." In this regard, Zola's conclusion to *J'Accuse* "has a disturbing parallel to Edouard Drumont's vicious anti-Semitic article, 'The Soul of Captain Dreyfus.' " Sennett emphasizes the similarities in the self-dramatization of the author and the dehumanization of the enemy, in which the essential goal is to define irreconcilable communities, and thus he reads the affair as typified by "inward turning language[,] . . . rigidity for the sake of feeling bound up in the group, a defiance of the dissonances of history for the sake of community." For Sennett, the substance of the Dreyfus case, the questions of truth or falsity regarding the facts of the matter, are of negligible interest; the innocence of Dreyfus is indubitable but insignificant.[14]

This is also the approach that informs Richard Griffiths's work *The Use of Abuse: The Polemics of the Dreyfus Affair and Its Aftermath*, in which the essential meaning of the affair is to be read in the violent, irresponsible, and politically pernicious polemic of both camps. "What we now see as a judicial mistake," he writes, "compounded by fears of admitting that a mistake had been made, and then further compounded by fears of the forces that had thus been released, became transformed into a straightforward battle between uncompromising enemies." Passing over Griffiths's rhetorical technique—which subsumes under "judicial mistake" that entire panoply of illegal procedures, fabrications, forgeries, false claims about foreign intervention, the railroading of Picquart, and the sheltering of Esterhazy—I wish to emphasize his focus on the meaning of the affair in the rhetoric of its antagonists. Griffiths grants that "when it came to personal vilification . . . the anti-Dreyfusards were on the whole more vile and more violent than most of their opponents," but in most respects, he argues, this was a matter of degree, as the actual techniques applied were similar. From this point he concludes that the two camps were virtually indistinguishable in contributing to the deterioration of political discourse in France. Griffiths's emphasis is on the results: "both sides in the Affair, carried away with their own rhetoric, lost hold on reality and created a new 'reality' of their own—leaving far behind them the case itself, and its unfortunate victim."[15]

The considerable literature that locates the meaning of the affair in its pernicious consequences has come to no consensus on which consequences were the most pernicious. One familiar theme has to do with the pernicious effects on the army and therefore French security in the light of the cosmic conflicts of the twentieth century. The hostility toward the officer corps, its persecution when the Dreyfusards were in the political saddle, and the general tension between a segment of the political elite and the armed forces are blamed for the striking incompetence of the military leaders of the French response to the German invasion in 1914 (somewhat less incompetent than its response to the invasions in 1870 and 1940). The military historian Douglas Porch carries this line right up to the fall of France in the Second World War: "When defeat seemed certain in 1940, a generation of soldiers who had suffered arrogant politicians since 1900 did not pass up the opportunity to pull the rug from under the feet of its tormentors."[16]

In an article entitled "The Dreyfus Affair and the Corruption of the French Legal System," Benjamin Martin presents a "more complicated and less moralistic" assessment of the corruptions of the judicial process than the standard unqualified condemnation of the implacable persecution of a victim of anti-Semitism by a self-serving military elite. Martin grants the shameful irregularity of the proceedings of the first military tribunal and the ludicrous verdict of the second, both of which condemned Dreyfus on the basis of illegally submitted and fabricated evidence, but he goes on to argue that "many of the Dreyfusards acted out of a determination to right an injustice, only to commit injustice themselves in the process. Eventually, for both sides, the ends justified the means. And few on either side appeared to understand when damage to principle was done the legal system was politicized."

Martin's "more complicated and less moralistic" account honors the Dreyfusards for their courageous battle for justice in a legal system that was often and even characteristically unjust, but he also reads the motives of the military leaders in a more or less sympathetic light and emphasizes the deplorable results of overturning an illegal decision, "however improper," by legislation rather than by another legal decision.[17]

One can find a virtually paradigmatic presentation of the line that treats Dreyfus's innocence as assumed, but more or less beside the historical point, in Theodore Zeldin's influential and idiosyncratic work *The History of France, 1848 to 1945*. Like Griffiths and Martin, Zeldin recommends Douglas Johnson's book as "the most judicious and perceptive study" and in a brief compass rings virtually all of the changes on what might be called the "modified revisionist theme with special emphasis on consequences." In Zeldin's reading the Dreyfusard intellectuals set France back thirty years by "refusing to let it go forward in the solution of the problems of the day." Thus the affair itself "was one of the greatest failures of the Republic, precisely because it impeded advance beyond the disputes of the nineteenth century."[18] Zeldin isn't clear as to what would have constituted an advance beyond the disputes of the nineteenth century, and indeed, one might remark that the Dreyfusards were actually mired in such shibboleths of the eighteenth century as the Declaration of the Rights of Man, whereas people on the other side, such as Maurras and Barrès, looked forward to the twentieth century in rhetorical anticipations of fascism.

One common theme in the modern "less moralistic" school of interpretation is the application of the principle of *tout comprendre*, if not quite *tout pardonner*, to an empathetic reconstruction of the motives of the conventional "villains" of the story, to right the balance against the anachronistic sanctification of the heroes. Their emphasis on consequences rather than truth does indeed rethink past thought, as the affirmation of consequences was at the very rhetorical and moral core of the anti-Dreyfusard camp. Yet this emphasis *is* anachronistic, because coming to terms with the facts of the *case* was inseparable from the establishment of a partisan identity in either camp.

One could read as the implicit message of those historians who dwell on deplorable consequences of insisting on the truth that during the affair it would have been better, if not expressly to lie, at least not to have insisted so zealously on the truth. Or perhaps this is too doctrinaire an interpretation. Some of them grant the virtue of that first cohort of truth-tellers, sometimes labeled Dreyfusists, who at considerable cost dedicated themselves to asserting an ideal, in contrast to the Dreyfusards, who subsequently exploited the affair.

The canonical version of this interpretation was articulated by Charles Péguy in 1910.[19] It seems impossible to write a piece on the affair without citing his aphorism about how *mystique* degenerated into *politique*. According to some commentators, this degeneration into the *politique*—the illiberal treatment of religion, the tendentious purges of the officer corps, and so forth—is a negative reflection back on the original crusade; but Péguy refused to believe that the subsequent corruption of the ideal forced a reevaluation of that heroic mystique as a tragic mystification. Péguy's work *Notre Jeunesse* was composed as a specific refutation of an erstwhile Dreyfusist who looked back on the days of that great struggle with an ambivalence that could be interpreted as regret. This was Daniel Halévy, Péguy's close friend and comrade-in-arms, whose work "Apologie pour notre passé"[20] was read by Péguy as an *apology* for their commitment to the cause, in light of its dismal effects. Actually, Péguy's long, impassioned response, perhaps the best-remembered of all his works, is an example of interpretive overkill, since what Halévy wrote was an apologia, a *justification* for the commitment to the battle to free Dreyfus, despite the subsequent corruption of the ideal. Péguy's essential objection referred to the least hint that the Dreyfusists, whose eternal glory dwelt in that first heroic commitment to truth and justice, might in any sense share the responsibility for its degeneration into the politique of the opportunistic Dreyfusards; "my past," he said, "needs no apology."[21]

While he enumerated in obsessive, eloquent detail the pernicious consequences of the corruption of the original mystique, Péguy would not enter a negative balance: the temporal balance sheet, the *salut temporel*, of the nation, weighed as nothing against the *salut eternel*. The immortal soul of France had been saved by the Dreyfusists. According to the conventional wisdom, the *cité* did not depend on the fate of a single citizen, and yet one single crime, one example of injustice, if officially sanctioned and universally accepted, will fracture the social contract and dishonor an entire people.[22]

Thus Péguy never would concede to the anti-Dreyfusards the argument about the consequences—an argument that would be central to the response to the Dreyfus case once a specter of doubt was raised by that handful of revisionists. At that point the question of consequences became the guiding principle of the political elite, who simply wanted to bury this issue, which could only have unfortunate and divisive results.

As the Dreyfusard chorus swelled, it became difficult to argue this line without reference to the truth of the original charge—that is, difficult for political pragmatists of a certain stripe, then as now, simply to say, "It is meet and right to lie in a good cause." It would take the malevolent ingenuity of Charles Maurras to create a cult of the heroic lie when the forgery of Colonel Henry was exposed, and even that was supposed to be the authentic copy of verbal communications.

The version of truth that proceeds from the argument from authority, dominant at first in the rational deference to the decision of the military court, was transformed into a transcendent faith in the integrity of the officer caste, invulnerable to any appeal to evidence or logic.

After the public exposure of facts that undermined the presumption of guilt, a far different appeal to authority appeared in a *Manifesto of the Intellectuals* in Clemenceau's journal *L'Aurore*, in the issue that published Zola's *J'Accuse*. The collective endorsement of this outrageous attack on the military elite as perpetrators of a judicial crime was immediately perceived as a claim that depended on the prestige of spokesmen for high culture. And the answer was the organization of a competing group of writers and thinkers, leading to that confrontation of the "families" of the intelligentsia, a subject on which there is a substantial body of literature.[23] I do not intend to reexplore the ground so well covered by Stephen Wilson, Christopher Charle, and others in drawing sociological or disciplinary profiles of these groups, but I do wish to reexamine the claims to authority and the criteria of truth that developed out of their debate.

The manifesto of the intellectuals was greeted with outrage, not only for its content but also for its presumption, attacked in language that is familiar enough in our day and, as in our day, by people we would identify as other intellectuals. The masterful vituperation of Maurice Barrès is often cited at this point. The use of the term "intellectual" was bad enough, he wrote, but nothing was worse than the thing itself. The culture of the soi-disant intellectuals was a "demi-culture" that ruined instinct without replacing it by conscience. "All of these aristocrats of the mind insist on proclaiming that they do not think like the vile multitude. . . . They no longer sense their affinity with their natural kind and do not attain the clairvoyance that would recover a conscious identity with the masses."[24]

Another virtually magisterial anathema leveled against writers and academics with political presumption, less remembered now but carrying a great authority then, was that of Ferdinand Brunetière—himself a mandarin among the mandarins. Brunetière was a professor and a public figure, an immensely influential if controversial literary historian and critic, a professor at the *École normale*, his career crowned by a chair in the *Académie française*. He was also editor of the *Revue des Deux Mondes*, where he published his personal manifesto "Après le procès [the Zola trial]" in the issue of March 15, 1898. After what might most charitably be described as an equivocal treatment of anti-Semitism and a paean to the French army, Brunetière turned with heavy sarcasm to the pretensions of this self-identified group of so-called intellectuals. "What conception of life," Brunetière asks, "granted them the authority to lord over those who didn't honor that designation?" According to what criterion was this prestigious title awarded to distinguished paleographers or linguists or scientists? By what right was the actual distinction acquired in some particular field of study presumed to extend to whatever area these professors were inclined to consider? Such "grand words" as "scientific method, aristocracy of the intelligence, respect for truth" simply concealed the pretensions of individuals and capitalized and underlined the great contemporary malady, in which "each of us . . . sets himself up as sovereign judge of everything." Brunetière's special targets were the experts presuming an authority outside of their disciplines, as in the case of the paleographer who presumed to refute "the judgment of three court martials"—that is, such distinguished scholars as Paul Meyer, director of the *École Nationale des Chartes*, who testified at the Zola trial. In effect, such a self-infatuated individualism approaches anarchy, and it is clear enough where that leads. In an earlier passage Brunetière had made the point that "the discipline indispensable to the existence of armies is precisely and uniquely incompatible with individualism and with anarchy." The army, the great bulwark and incarnation of French democracy, had found its worst enemy in those so-called intellectuals.[25]

Brunetière's manifesto constituted a public challenge, and it was immediately taken up, notably by fellow academics directly or implicitly condemned by his diatribe. The response of Émile Durkheim remains of considerable interest because it documents his location on the political spectrum and because he strikes chords characteristic of arguments advanced by Brunetière's adversaries. Durkheim vigorously defends the individualism that is the central target of Brunetière's tirade. Like Péguy, if not in his apocalyptic language, Durkheim reverses the nationalist thesis about consequences of the public exercise of independent judgment: "Not only is individualism not anarchical, but it henceforth is the only system of belief which can insure the moral unity of the country."[26] In effect, individualism conceived as freedom of expression is a unifying characteristic of Durkheim's France, an indispensable constituent of the national identity. To restrict it is to compromise the national existence. A far different France might have emerged from an affair in which the Dreyfusard truth had been repressed and the ultranationalist version of the affair affirmed.

This reading of the implications of the affair retains its contemporary relevance. Those historians who conclude that to be a Dreyfusard was to prefer some ideal of the truth over the health of the state have preempted the argument as to consequences. Even to say that the affair became a myth, whether or not in the pejorative sense, is to say something about the society that France became, to note an entry in the register of the French people's collective memory, to specify the constituents of their political culture. The anti-Semitic strain that polluted political discourse in France even before the affair would never prevail; France would not go fascist in the 1930s and would only succumb to the tradition incarnated in the other camp as a result of the defeat of 1940.[27]

Durkheim also came to grips with Brunetière's attack on intellectuals' presumptuous claims to general authority. Durkheim's response was to become the familiar justification of the intellectual *engagé*: to enjoy the right and assume the duty to participate, as any other citizen, in public discourse. With reference to the issue at hand, Durkheim argued,

> To know whether a tribunal can be permitted to condemn an accused man without having heard his defense requires no special intelligence. It is a problem of practical ethics for which every man of good sense is competent and to which no one should be indifferent. If, therefore, in recent times, a certain number of artists, and especially scholars, believed they had to refuse to concur in a judgment whose legality appeared to them suspect, it was not because in their capacity as chemists or philologists, as philosophers or historians, they attributed to themselves some sort of special privilege and a sort of eminent right of control over the thing being judged. It is because, being men, they intend to exercise all their human rights and retain before them a matter which is amenable to reason alone.[28]

This unexceptionable statement does leave something unsaid. The signers of the *Manifesto of the Intellectuals* and subsequent collections of signatures were not randomly distributed along the population of the Dreyfusards. There we find the names of Émile Zola, Anatole France, Daniel Halévy, Marcel Proust, Gabriel Monod, Charles Seignobos, Lucien Herr, and so forth, not a selection of modest *instituteurs*, Jewish laborers, or anticlerical peasants. The critics of the manifesto rightly sensed some claim to collective authority. Indeed, Durkheim suggests this in the sentences following his assertion of the rights that intellectuals shared with all men because of their common humanity: "It is true that they have shown themselves to be more jealous of that right than has the rest of the society; but it is simply because in consequence of their professional practices they take it more to heart. Since they are accustomed by the practice of the scientific method to reserve their judgment as long as they do not feel themselves enlightened, it is natural that they should yield less easily to the sway of the masses and the prestige of authority."[29]

"The practice of the scientific method": from the ultraskeptical perspective of the end of our century, when authority is denied even to scientists speaking within their own disciplines, when the ideal of the scientific method is characterized as an ideology of dominance, when the Enlightenment has been written off as a "failure," what legitimacy is left to the civic pretensions of a scientific (or social scientific) *Weltanschauung*? And at the end of the last century the other side had its scientists, too, claiming the authority that anthropometrists and social Darwinists conferred on bigotry and racism.[30] However, the pretension that their conclusions were illuminated by the light of science was much more a weapon in the revisionists' arsenal, so it became a target for the facile contempt of their antagonists. Thus Ferdinand Brunetière, who had already demolished to his satisfaction the cosmic pretensions of science in general, turned his guns on the presumption that expertise in the physical sciences endowed anyone with the authority to speak on political or legal issues and on the idea that the methods of the social scientists applied to matters of disputable fact had anything to do with scientific demonstration or formal proof.[31]

As Maurice Blanchot remarks in his "Les Intellectuels en question," such an objection can be applied generally to intellectuals' presumption that their specific expertise entitles them to an authority over subjects for which they have no special competence. In fact, Blanchot says, this is not necessarily an unreasonable assumption to the extent that intellectuals apply the quality of mind that has won them distinction, rather than as they too often do, assuming the authority while applying slipshod methods they would never accept in their professional pursuits.[32]

In fact, the Dreyfusist savants who appealed to the model of the scientific method in political debate—the chemists Edouard Grimaux or Émile Duclaux, for example—did not claim either the authority of their professional distinction or the authority of what passes for proof in the physical sciences. Their essential appeal was not to a specific disciplinary method but to a professional ethic transferred to the realm of public affairs.[33]

This was an ethic that could be practiced by anyone. As Duclaux, director of the Institut Pasteur and one of the participants in the running debate with Brunetière, put it, "What is scientific reasoning? Quite simply, reasoning applied with the healthy fear of self-deception and the resolution to avoid it." Irrespective of scholarly discipline, from physicist to historian, "all are worthy of the title of savant on condition that they do their research with integrity, *sans parti pris*, and find the evidence for their conclusions outside of themselves, independent of the subjective realm where the hypothesis to be verified was born."[34]

The appropriation of the authority of objectivity, *sans parti pris*, was the familiar language of the revisionists in public debate and at the major trials.[35] To be without bias in this sense is not equivalent to neutrality; the *engagement* of the Dreyfusard savant was scarcely value-free. But among the values implicit in the Dreyfusards' assertion of objectivity was the commitment to apply one's best standards, one's most rigorous criteria of truth, to the issue in question irrespective of other preferences or personal costs.

And there were indeed personal costs, especially in the early stages of the struggle. The distinguished chemist Edouard Grimaux, who took the stand at the Zola struggle to defend his honor as a bred-in-the-bone patriot, forced against the grain to conclude that the leadership of his beloved army had failed their country, would stick to his guns despite dismissal from his chair at the École Polytechnique, repudiation by sometime friends and colleagues, and vilification and physical harassment at public meetings.[36]

Still, to suffer for an ideal is not to guarantee its authenticity. Furthermore, the experts who testified for the other side at the trials also claimed the authority of inference from indubitable evidence *sans parti pris*. While some anti-Dreyfusard polemicists gloried in their lack of objectivity, most continued to insist that the original decision of the court martial was, in fact, correct.[37] However, the appeals to common evidential standards concealed a crucial difference. A Durkheim or a Duclaux continued to assume the possible falsifiability of his conclusions, in or out of the laboratory, whereas the anti-Dreyfusards merely exploited that ethic: that is, faced with convincing, and eventually devastating, evidence that not Dreyfus but Esterhazy was the spy, they tacitly exploited the proposition that no accumulation of evidence about matters of fact is the equivalent of a formal proof. The apprehension that it is always possible to imagine some additional fact that might falsify a given conclusion encouraged the proliferation of lies by unscrupulous demagogues like Rochefort; the elaborate graphological analyses intended to explain away the fact that the handwriting of the *bordereau* seemed closer to that of Ester-hazy than of Dreyfus; or, as in Figueras's recent book, the suggestion that all of the documents exposed as indubitable forgeries had been planted by agents of the Dreyfusard cabal to discredit the counterintelligence apparatus. In practice, the antirevisionist appeal to the facts of the case has never been separated from the pragmatic principle that truth is what serves the cause. That is why Daniel Hoffman is right to distinguish the critical rationalism of the Dreyfusard tradition (despite obvious individual deviations) from the systematic lies of its antagonists.

Admittedly, my citation of the Dreyfusard scientists or Durkheim is selective, tailored to support an argument. In making a different argument, Richard Griffiths chooses to emphasize the nasty polemics of Urban Gohier and Laurent Tailhade, scarcely first-rank luminaries in the Dreyfusard galaxy. It is not my intention to select out exemplary Dreyfusards as representative figures or to fabricate a rationalist saints-calendar, but to examine the criteria of commitment to the cause insofar as those criteria constituted a response to the facts of the case.

The commitment to rationalism and objectivity is, as we are now often reminded, the product of historical circumstance and is, I would agree, a moral choice. Those who reject that choice presumably embrace another, although it is difficult to find someone engaged in a morally charged debate about the past who publicly repudiates rational standards—not to speak of simply admitting to lying in a good cause. Even Maurice Barrès, who assimilated standards of truth to group loyalties, never admitted to lying about the case in the conventional sense of the term.

There is one rather odd exception to this inhibition: the writer Paul Léautaud. Léautaud contributed to the Henry Memorial, *Le Monument Henry*, organized by an anti-Semitic journal in support of the widow of the martyred forger, and accompanied his contribution with the comment "Pour l'ordre, contre la justice et la vérité." It is difficult to know what to make of this— perhaps that sort of mischievousness that the French call *gaminerie*. Léautaud identified himself as a Dreyfusard and cheerfully engaged in arguments over the affair with his friend Paul Valéry, who had made his contribution to the Henry Memorial accompanied by the inexpungible "non sans réflexion."[38]

Valéry never retreated from that early indiscretion, and he persisted in an attitude toward the affair and the truth about the affair that I will label "aesthetic," in Allan Megill's sense of aestheticism as "a tendency to see 'art' or 'language' or 'discourse' or 'text' as constituting the primary realm of human experience,"[39] applying it in this case to moral judgment. After the association of the term "aesthetic" with political morality occurred to me, I came upon the controversy over the wartime writings of Paul de Man, in which the "aestheticizing" of politics is presumed, on the authority of Walter Benjamin, to lend itself to, or even be the essence of, fascism. This is not the place to detail what I think is wrong with all of that;[40] I simply want to characterize the tendency to disassociate political commitment and moral judgment from any conception of truth.

The aesthetic approach in the most narrow and literal sense was expressed with characteristic flippant cynicism by Léon Daudet, major star in the Pleiades of the *Action Française* and an implacable enemy of the Dreyfus ideal until his death in 1942, who once described Dreyfusism as "a lesion that infects everything, even aesthetic judgment. There is a Dreyfusard hue."[41]

With Valéry the issue is somewhat more complex. Marcel Thomas's assemblage of the fragmentary evidence about Valéry's refusal to withdraw from a position that became less defensible with the passage of years traces out Valéry's transition from a belligerence that drove André Gide into craven apologies for having signed the *Manifesto of the Intellectuals* to scattered, more or less defensive allusions to that remote historic moment.[42] None of these published and unpublished scraps suggest a conviction that Dreyfus was in fact a traitor. At the time of the affair, Valéry's justification proceeded from an argument as to consequences. The affair contributed to the erosion of power at the center, the quasi-anarchy of "counter powers," the self-promotion of mediocrities, the strain on "the mechanism of the army already so delicate in a democratic country."

In Valéry's last recorded reflections on the affair, his justification is no longer cast as a political, but rather as a personal, response to the behavior of the Dreyfusards:

> Not "wicked"—that is to say feeling pain at the sight of pain—yet my heart feels no pity for anyone who exploits my compassion—or who tries to gain his ends through invocations to Justice, Humanity, etc. So much so that, in

spite of his appeals to established Idols, I align myself with Injustice and take refuge in the disgust at this comedy, of which I have seen many examples. That explains my attitude during the celebrated Affair. For one does not become a man simply by invoking Humanity—I knew those men who were exempt from no human weakness and no weakness of the man of letters—and in this particular case I saw them inflame themselves and others for a cause.[43]

As Blanchot remarks after quoting this passage, "Pénible souvenir, pénible énigme."[44] All the more enigmatic in the light of Valéry's reputation as an icon of lucidity and rationality.[45] In this case the standards are neither rational or pragmatic but set by rhetorical sensibility. Presumably the self-righteous discourse of the self-proclaimed intellectuals, the "stupidity and false bonhomie of such 'savants' as Duclaux, Reville, etc.,"[46] justify the embrace of injustice. The moral touchstone for Valéry, as for such subsequent commentators as Sennett and Griffiths, is not the truth about matters of contested fact but the quality of the contestants' discourse.

Not that Valéry, even in his militant phase, expressed solidarity with demagogues like Drumont or Rochefort. The aesthetic stance is usually characterized by a certain degree of "a plague on both your houses." This is the case with Romain Rolland, who acquired an unsolicited Dreyfusard reputation because his play *Les Loups* was understood, contrary to his intentions, as a revisionist allegory. Rolland, an anti-Semite with a Jewish wife, believed that both sets of protagonists of the affair, which he considered a tragic conflict of valid principles, were infected with corrupt motives. Therefore he took a stand "above the battle": "When a house is on fire each one saves what is most precious to him, for some it was justice; for others the tradition of *la patrie*. For me it was reason."

Rolland's version of "reason" spoke not to the facts of the case or to the issue of Dreyfus's innocence (of which he was apparently convinced) but to the unreasonable behavior, the "fanaticism," of the contending parties. After the Henry forgery, he reaffirmed his anti-Semitic inclinations, which he would have set aside, he assured Lucien Herr, "if justice hadn't remained quite secondary in the preoccupations of the defenders of Dreyfus."[47] As if it were a matter of taste, observes Blanchot[48]—even of literary taste. Rolland told Lucien Herr that he would support neither a dubious cause nor "a writer whose character I have never esteemed."

The writer was almost certainly Zola. Zola's role as the heroic voice of justice never has been universally celebrated. The bombastic and self-dramatizing rhetoric of *J'Accuse* is not much to modern taste and received mixed reviews at the time. For example, after Georges Sorel's disenchantment by the corruption of the original mystique had transformed him from a combative Dreyfusard into a malicious critic of the paladins of Dreyfusism, he characterized Zola as the "representative man of the buffoonery of this era." Even Joseph Reinach had to admit, says Sorel, that *J'Accuse* was a collection of "romantic bric-a-brac applied without taste and without moderation" and Zola's trial testimony "one of those absurd and sonorous speeches of the sort delivered by one of Victor Hugo's characters."[49]

I have not cited this passage to suggest that the reason for the radical change in Sorel's attitude toward the affair was aesthetic; it proceeded from the outrage he shared with Péguy at the degeneration of the original ideals into the sordid maneuvers of the republican politicos. But unlike Péguy, Sorel responded to the degeneration of the ideal by casting a negative light backward onto the entire meaning of the affair. The structure of his tract *La Révolution Dreyfusienne* is cast in the form of a vast argument ad hominem in which Sorel compares the affair to the French Revolution, characterizing both moments through the discrepancy between the historical immensity of the events and the pitiful shrunken moral stature of their protagonists. This interpretation is applied in detail to the Dreyfusard heroes—Zola, Anatole France, Jaurès, and even Colonel Picquart. No conjecture or innuendo about corrupt motive is overlooked in "Sorel's most deplorable publication."[50]

Wherever Sorel took his stand, it could not have been on the ground occupied by a Durkheim or a Jaurès. His hostility to rationalism as a principle of intellectual existence and to professional intellectuals as bearers of the rationalist virus, of "the metaphysics of the people who vulgarized the vulgarization of the eighteenth century,"[51] guaranteed that his political stance would not depend on conventional criteria regarding the truth value of statements about contestable facts.

Shortly before the First World War, at the time of Sorel's flirtation with ultraroyalism and an affectation of vicious anti-Semitism,[52] he wrote to the *Action Française* that he was stimulated by the hostility of the Dreyfusards to wonder whether "I should not now write a brochure on the reasons that would lead one to believe in the treason of Alfred Dreyfus."[53] I read this not as an assertion of Sorel's conviction that Dreyfus was in fact guilty as charged but as a suggestion of what the Dreyfusards had coming to them.

In his anti-Dreyfusard phase, Sorel damned the Dreyfusards for the consequences of their agitation, which weakened the "social structure," that is, the coalition of elites that enabled the parliamentary system to function—a rather odd objection for that sometime Pied Piper of the general strike.[54] In any phase, Sorel was never concerned with the objective validity of a movement's ideology but with how it worked, and at this time his transcending of rational or empirical criteria in political conflict aligned him with the pragmatic and irrationalist ethic of Charles Maurras and Maurice Barrès, who would transform anti-Dreyfusard politics into a permanent protofascist *politique*.

Charles Maurras, whose celebration of Colonel Henry's patriotic forgery was the launching pad for a lifetime career as philosophic guru of the ultranationalist Right, asserted the categorical priority of the pragmatic standard. "I do not wish to reengage in the old debate, *innocent* or *guilty*," he wrote. What mattered was the damage inflicted on France by the defenders of Dreyfus. "Unfortunately societies without justice have been seen, but one has yet to see justice without a society." But Maurras's pragmatism never inhibited his appeal to the "evidence" of Dreyfus's guilt, such as the claim that Esterhazy, "straw man of the Jews," had been paid to imitate the handwriting in the *bordereau*.[55]

This is the case too of Maurice Barrès, the most brilliantly perverse polemicist in the antirevisionist camp then and ever since. Barrès was a figure of considerable literary and political influence before the First World War; his novels became a generational touchstone for the educated youth of the 1890s. Although he was subject to the ferocious contempt of the postwar intelligentsia, he has remained an admired figure for the French Right, but the primary revival of interest in his work during the last two decades has been in his presumed role as a precursor of fascism. There is no complete consensus on this, but the works of Ernst Nolte, Robert Soucy, C. Doty, and especially Zeev Sternhell have made a strong case for the anticipations of fascism in Barrès's fiction and in the polemical journalism hammered out during his battle against the Dreyfusards. According to Nolte, Barrès propounded "a relativist irrationalism—obviously a position of decadence—[that] glorifies instinct and blood and thus creates one of the most remarkable characterizations of future fascism."[56]

I wish to emphasize an element of the Barrèsian polemic that was indeed characteristic of fascist ideology but that also has a quite contemporary resonance. This is his location of truth or the criteria for truth in a community and its presumed interests.

Although Barrès' pugnacious assault on the Dreyfusard camp came as a surprise to many of his young acolytes on the Left,[57] Zeev Sternhell and others have persuasively analyzed the continuity in his ideas that made his anti-Dreyfusism continuous with attitudes already affirmed, notably in his extremely influential novel *Les Déracinés*. In this novel published on the eve of the outbreak of the affair, Barrès depicts a Kantian professor engaged in poisoning the minds of the novel's young protagonists through his version of the categorical imperative: "I ought always to act such that I would wish that my action was the universal rule."[58] Rather than demand the regurgitation of such lifeless abstractions, it was necessary to teach a particular truth rooted in a particular environment and a certain human community. It was necessary to teach "French truth, that is to say, that which is most useful to the nation." "Les préjugés nationaux" were the very stuff of wisdom.[59]

This was the version of truth that would turn out to be appropriate to anti-Dreyfusard polemic—indeed, providential, once the evidence about the fabricated indictment began to accumulate. Barrès's assertion "It is hopeless to try to establish truth solely by reason, since the mind can always find a new reason to question the conclusions"[60] forecasts generations of dialectical acrobats who continued to invent one more scenario designed to assimilate and explain away the manifest evidence about the overwhelming probability of the innocence of the accused. But for Barrès the unassailable redoubt would be his definition of truth as "French," rooted in the soil where his ancestors were interred, inaccessible to Protestants or Jews, and the unassailable authority for the refutation of opposing views. Thus Émile Zola could be disposed of with reference to his Venetian descent, which guaranteed a mentality alien to that of the French.[61] Proust's Baron Charlus carries the Barrèsian logic to its ultimate conclusion when he observes that "in any case the crime is non-existent. This compatriot [Dreyfus] of your friend would have committed a crime if he had betrayed Judaea, but what has he to do with France?"[62]

Barrès's ethnocentric standard of truth might now be read as an affirmation of solidarity in Richard Rorty's sense,[63] although Barrès preferred the term "affinity" to "solidarity" because he wanted to emphasize the instinctual feelings of sympathy and identity inherited from the past and transmitted in the blood.[64] This is scarcely the sort of solidarity that Rorty has in mind; nor, presumably, what those who relativize truth to the standards of particular communities intend. "Tribalism" is the term applied to the Barrès version.[65] One might say that, projecting our own tribal sympathies into the past, we liberals would have belonged to some other tribe, by choice rather than birth—that of Jaurès or Anatole France—and in accepting their standards of truth, then as now, would have had no dialogue with Barrès except the discourse of combat.

This is certainly the way that Barrès claimed to see it. Implacable opponents face each other across impassable barriers, not merely of political preference but of incommensurable standards of veridicality. But this was not, in fact, the case. The contesting "tribes" inhabited the same time and space, shared the same political, social, and human circumstances, and partook of the same tradition of intelligible discourse. Here I borrow the burden of Ernest Gellner's critique of Peter Winch's anthropological relativism, where he argues that radically distinct societies often overlap.[66] Just as the Aztecs and Spaniards who confronted each other on the causeway outside of Tenochtitlán shared a flesh vulnerable to missiles, irrespective of their respectively viable systems of myth or science, so the combatants in that small French arena all faced the insistent question of the actual guilt or innocence of Captain Dreyfus. Undoubtedly they approached that question out of the matrix of prior loyalties and other assumptions: there was the old radical who allegedly said that all he needed to know was where the priests and generals stood in order to locate himself in the other camp; or Paul Claudel, who wrote that he could not deny his mother—that is, the insults of foreign commentators on the affair aligned him on the side of France and against the Jews.[67] But this is not to say that the arguments of the contending parties were incommensurable, as if they actually spoke different languages.

This is the case with Barrès himself, who was never willing to concede the epistemological terrain of conventional argument to the Dreyfusards. Thus, in order to justify deference to the duly constituted authority of the military court, he argues the lack of sufficient information through which the layman could evaluate the facts of the case. This appeal to the authority of the *vérité judiciaire* as opposed to any "absolute truth" was to make a conventional appeal to an authority that we respect because it knows what it is talking about, is professionally competent and uniquely in command of relevant information. In addition, Barrès never hesitated to summon up the hard evidence that was to demonstrate Dreyfus's guilt to any rational intellect. In reporting on the Rennes trial he returned to the "demonstration" that the crime could only have been committed by a gunner assigned to the general staff as a *stagiaire*, and he still evoked the expertise of Bertillon, who produced "before the council of war the same geometric technique that Dreyfus employed" to disguise his own handwriting. For this particular performance Bertillon had literally been laughed out of court, even by many of the anti-Dreyfusards. The continued celebration, long after the event, of Bertillon's "genius" by Barrès, Charles Maurras, and Léon Daudet is an indicator of the ethical quality of a historical discourse that never dispensed with the cynical exploitation of whatever seemed to do the polemical job.[68]

Despite the appeals to those conventional standards of objectivity that Barrès was to relativize out of existence on suitable occasions, Lucien Herr was right when he said that the question of innocence or guilt, of justice or legal crime, was of no moment to Barrès.[69] He could not help but speak the same language as the Dreyfusard intelligentsia in debate about the actual bearings of the case, but he spoke it without scruple. And here he does belong to a different community, defined in terms not of language but of morality.

I do not believe that one can grant the facts of the Dreyfus case as a more or less insignificant given in order to emphasize the political rhetoric attendant on the affair, not because I believe that the rhetorical element is negligible but because the language in which the conflict was cast was imbued with claims to knowledge of what had actually occurred. The truth of the case was central, not marginal, to the affair. That is why I disagree with Johnson and Sennett and Griffiths, who conflate the rhetorical excesses of the contending camps. That is why I think Richard Griffiths and Michael Marrus[70] are wrong to assimilate the Dreyfusard fabrication of the Jesuit conspiracy to the anti-Dreyfusard figment of the Jewish Syndicate. The former was a familiar weapon seized by the more unscrupulous Dreyfusards,[71] the latter an indispensable instrument of a polemic forced to explain away the accumulation of embarrassing facts. The Dreyfusard tactic of publishing copies of relevant documents was scarcely available to the other camp. Not even the evocation of Colonel Henry's heroic act of patriotic forgery would do the job. Eventually it would be necessary to invent and reinvent that implacable organization which had even planted false documents in Dreyfus's dossier in order to undermine the valid indictment.

It is true that the motives of the Dreyfusards ranged from disinterested to corrupt and that the testimony about their commitment is often self-serving, but many people did join the movement, some at considerable personal inconvenience and risk, only after they were convinced of the truth according to their lights. And many of the opportunists shifted sides only after the truth became so apparent to common sense that a different sort of commitment was required to continue to insist on Dreyfus's guilt. Faced with the fact that Dreyfus was indeed innocent, the anti-Dreyfusards would hit on a criterion of "truth" that subsumes what are ordinarily called lies, and that is not their least significant anticipation of a fascist politics.

Those scholars and scientists such as Durkheim and Grimaux who associated the ethic of their discipline with their public values were not asserting a sort of political scientism but applying what John Dewey called "the spirit of scientific inquiry" to public life. Their values are well characterized by Richard Bernstein's description of Dewey's ethos:

> It is the openness of scientific inquiry, the imagination required for its successful practice, the willingness to submit a hypothesis to public test and criticism, the intrinsic communal and cooperative character of scientific inquiry that Dewey highlighted when he spoke of "scientific method." If we are to dedicate ourselves to the task of the concrete realization of "creative democracy," then, it is these virtues that must be cultivated and nurtured in our everyday moral and political lives.[72]

These were the virtues to which the best of the Dreyfusards appealed and the virtues that the anti-Dreyfusards, given the nature of their cause, were bound to subvert.

Chapter 3

No reading is conceivable in which the question of its truth or

falsehood is not primarily involved.—Paul de Man

The Debate over the Wartime Writings of Paul de Man: The Language of Setting the Record Straight

It has been argued that the historian's confidence in some stable, retrievable, representable past is fatally undermined by the recognition that the past can only be reconstructed in the present. One reading of Benedetto Croce's oft-quoted observation "Every true history is contemporary history" is that the past is a present construct; that historians constitute a new reality rather than represent a past one. In its most radical form such an approach leaves no room for surprises. In fact, unanticipated traces of the past do constantly emerge to reconstruct the present.

As far as we know, no one alive at the dawn of 1947 knew that in a cave north of the Dead Sea there lay preserved from decay a set of documents whose discovery would change our vision of a particular past and therefore transform the present. Until a certain time in the late nineteenth century no historian had "constructed" a history of the American Southwest that incorporated the knowledge of the enigmatic remains at Mesa Verde and Chaco Canyon. Once "discovered," those remarkable structures irreversibly transformed the history of the region. It is no longer intellectually reputable to write the history of the peoples of the Southwest as if those artifacts did not exist. Independent of contemporary assumptions or intentions, such traces have imposed a new interpretive agenda.

A historical surprise that is not likely to have as profound implications for the present and future as the discovery of the Dead Sea Scrolls or the traces of Anasazi civilization was the discovery that Paul de Man, a literary scholar and critic of international distinction, had written articles for the collaborationist press in Belgium in 1941 and 1942.[1] While the significance of this discovery is scarcely world- historical, its effect has been intense in a narrow but broadly influential community of academics, litterateurs, and intellectuals of a certain stripe.

The revelation of de Man's wartime behavior was immediately perceived as a scandal of sufficient interest to be featured in the national press. It was headlined in the *New York Times*, "Yale Scholar Wrote for Pro-Nazi News-paper."[2] There was a special poignancy in these revelations in 1987 as they followed upon de Man's untimely death just four years earlier. De Man's death had evoked a public expression of loss, a rare response to the demise of a scholar whose life was cloistered and whose influence was felt most strongly in circles practicing an especially arcane intellectual discipline. Public ceremonies at Yale and elsewhere revealed not only respect for a creative scholar but something amounting to veneration for the personal qualities of a teacher whose intellectual austerity was felt as moral rectitude.[3]

Paul de Man was born in 1919 to a well-to-do and cultured Flemish family marked by the tragedy of the death of Paul's brother Hendrik in an accident in 1936 and the suicide of his mother a year later on the anniversary of Hendrik's death.[4] Paul would find something like a father surrogate in his uncle, Hendrik or Henri de Man,[5] one of the most influential figures in European socialism between the wars, and leader of the Belgian Workers' Party. On the eve of the Second World War, Henri entered the Belgian government and aligned himself with King Leopold in a policy of strict neutrality. When the German forces occupied Belgium in 1940, he dissolved his party and urged cooperation with the occupier. The significance of Paul's relation to his uncle remains the subject of considerable speculation.

In 1937 Paul de Man enrolled in the *Université Libre de Bruxelles* as a student first of engineering, then of chemistry. In 1939 his developing interests in politics and literature were reflected in his contributions to the student journals *Jeudi* and the *Cahiers du Libre Examen*, published by the *Cercle du Libre Examen*, which had been organized by a group of liberal and social democratic students opposed to fascist and communist totalitarianism. De Man probably edited the last two issues of the *Cahiers*, which ceased publication in February 1940, a few months before the German invasion of the Netherlands. During the invasion, de Man and Anaïde Baraghian, who was to become his wife, joined some two million Belgians in fleeing south. They reached the Pyrenees in May 1940, but after they were unable to obtain passage to Spain, they returned to Belgium, where de Man began to publish pieces on the literary-cultural scene in *Le Soir*, Belgium's major paper. Called *Le Soir volé* after it was expropriated by the Germans, it was edited by Belgians under the supervision of the Propaganda Abteilung of the Wehrmacht. De Man published in *Le Soir* between December 24, 1940, and November 29, 1942, and in a Flemish journal called *Het Vlaamsche Land* between March and October 1942. He was also employed by the *Bibliographie Dechenne*, the book distribution agency under German control, where he published brief bibliographical notices. He severed all connections with these publications in 1943 and apparently remained at his father's home in Antwerp until the end of the war.

Although identified as a turncoat and collaborationist after Belgium was liberated, a military court released him without filing charges. After an unsuccessful attempt to float a firm specializing in deluxe art books, he emigrated to New York, while his wife and two sons went to Argentina, where they intended to stay until they could join him in the United States. Through intellectual circles in New York he obtained a position as a French instructor at Bard College, married a Bard student, and apparently severed his relations with his first family. His evident brilliance and the quality of his literary essays earned him an appointment as a Junior Fellow at Harvard, though first he had to answer an anonymous accusation in a skillful letter claiming that he had stopped writing for *Le Soir* in 1941, when the Nazis imposed control over its contents: at that point, he claimed, he "did what was the duty of any decent person" (see Appendix A). From Harvard's Society of Fellows he was launched into a remarkable ascent through prestigious eastern universities, culminating in a professorship at Yale. There he became the center of a group of distinguished teachers and critics—possibly the first among peers—and at the time of his death arguably one of the most influential figures in what might be dignified as American high culture.

The revelations of de Man's collaborationist past were terribly distressing to friends, students, and a wide circle of admirers, and also immediately perceived as constituting a crisis with those associated with the literary-philosophical movement in which de Man was recognized, with Jacques Derrida, as the most significant voice. This movement is often crudely labeled "deconstructionism," and I will apply that term from time to time without pretending to some definitive definition.

Ortwin de Graef, the Belgian scholar who unearthed the wartime articles in the course of research on his doctoral thesis, immediately realized that he had uncovered a land mine. In August 1987, de Graef informed Jacques Derrida of the distressing discoveries. In October of that year, at a conference at the University of Alabama in Tuscaloosa, Derrida and a group of other scholars, many of whom were associated with the movement in which de Man was a central figure, decided to publish all of de Man's contributions during the occupation of Belgium—some 169 pieces for *Le Soir*, ten articles for the Flemish-language journal *Het Vlaamsche Land*, and book notes for the publishing house *Bibliographie Dechenne*, as well as his preinvasion contributions to student publications. In addition, thirty-eight literary theorists and other scholars responded to a request for reflections on the issue, and these essays were published in a volume entitled *Responses: On Paul de Man's Wartime Journalism*.[6]

The publication of the relevant documents by the people associated with de Man and deconstruction was intended to allow a more qualified and responsible treatment of the documents, even when they seemed to furnish ammunition to de Man's most biased detractors. Of course such intentions can be characterized as apologetic, but from the viewpoint of the conventional historian, the decision to publish everything was certainly laudable. The commitment to set the record straight seemed to supersede any sophisticated skepticism about the "transparency" of the recovered texts. Perhaps the facts wouldn't speak for themselves, but the publication of all of the evidence might preempt or constrain tendentious misreadings.

Indeed, by this time, "from one quarter, expressions of shock and dismay could be heard; from another, the distinctive note of *Schadenfreude*."[7] This is the characterization of David Lehman, himself damned as one of the loudest voices in the *Schadenfreude* chorus. Lehman's *Newsweek* piece on the de Man affair featured a photo of de Man and another of Nazi soldiers on the march and quoted the scholar and literary critic Jeffrey Mehlman to the effect that there are even "grounds for viewing the whole of deconstruction as a vast amnesty project for the politics of collaboration during World War II."[8]

While cheerfully questioning the motives of both the deconstructionists and their critics, Walter Kendrick's flippant piece in the *Village Voice*, "De Man That Got Away: Deconstructors on the Barricades," moved from de Man's shocking contribution to an anti-Semitic issue of *Le Soir* to the conclusion that "if Yale had required its Jewish students to wear a yellow star, no doubt Professor de Man would have gone on writing his dense and difficult essays."[9]

Historian Jon Wiener's article in the January 9, 1988, issue of the *Nation* provoked even more indignation than the contributions of Lehman and Kendrick. Referring to de Man as "something like an academic Waldheim" who had "successfully concealed his pro-Nazi past" after emigrating to the United States, Wiener unearthed other biographical details to add color, or smears, to a damning portrait: de Man had praised the work of the German literary critic Hans Robert Jauss, and "Jauss is now known to have served in the S.S." De Man also wrote a blurb for Julia Kristeva's *Powers of Horror*, which some have interpreted as sympathizing with Céline's anti-Semitism. It had become impossible, Wiener asserted, to read passages in de Man's later work "without thinking of de Man's collaboration." Some disreputable connection between the wartime writings and the contemporary literary movement labeled deconstruction was not precisely argued but was suggested through reference to damning comments on deconstruction by its critics.[10]

The description of Wiener's article as "rife with distortions and insinuations" was one of the milder responses to it. There was to be no concession to the slapdash rhetoric characteristic of muck-raking journalism. Indeed, Wiener himself would drop that approach and adopt the careful style of "responsible" argument as he responded to critics in the Letters section of the *Nation* and in a subsequent polemical exchange in *Critical Inquiry*.[11]

The angry answers to the "distortions" in the articles of Lehman, Wiener, and other journalistic accounts were early contributions to a running controversy in more or less popular publications, such as the *Nation*, the *Times Literary Supplement*, the *London Review of Books*, and the *Frankfurter Allgemeine Zeitung*, as well as in such specialized journals as *Critical Inquiry*. There Jacques Derrida published the flagship statement of the deconstructionists, "Like the Sound of the Sea Deep within a Shell: Paul de Man's War." A subsequent issue contained several critiques of Derrida's apologia and his long ferocious response to the critics.[12] The de Man affair furnished the matter for various think pieces—in the *New York Times Magazine*, for example—and then for chapters in books and essays in professional journals.[13]

All of this discussion inevitably produced a commentary on the controversy by the partisans themselves and by more or less dispassionate commentators. Most commentaries identify several distinct, if overlapping, issues. Here is my list: (1) a characterization and interpretation of what de Man actually wrote in the collaborationist press; (2) the implications for the evaluation of de Man as a human being—that is, for his posthumous reputation, with reference not only to his behavior during the war but also to why he concealed it; (3) the implications for reading de Man's immensely influential writings, for both evaluating and understanding them in the light of what preceded them; and (4) the implications of the writings of an author in his early twenties for an intellectual movement with which he was closely associated some thirty years later.

I am primarily concerned with the first issue—that is, with historical argument—although the question of how to judge de Man's life or work in the light of his past is certainly a historical issue. Much of *that* can be disposed of by way of Cornel West's remark "To use this profound moral lapse [de Man's wartime writings] to downplay de Man's later insights is sophomoric, just as to overlook it in the name of these insights is idolatrous,"[14] although things are a bit more complicated than that. There is already a dense hermeneutics on the relation between de Man's early writings and his mature oeuvre, and it is certainly legitimate to suppose that in some way or other the later work reflects his early concealed experience. On the other hand, anyone loyal to classic criteria of logical and temporal coherence would repudiate some prima facie condemnation of de Man's later writing because of what he wrote in his youth. The damning of deconstruction in the light of what de Man wrote thirty years prior to that movement seems an even more egregious non sequitur.

This tendentious and illogical projection of the past onto the present certainly fueled the indignation aroused by the journalistic exploitation of the scandal, but the defenders of de Man were also eager to refute misrepresentations of his wartime behavior and of his wartime writings. Their arguments to this effect were in turn harshly criticized as disingenuous special pleading.

As the controversy shifted from the columns of semipopular journals to the scholarly quarterlies, it became not less but more emotional. Though the academic teapot was small, the tempest was intense. Anger at the vindictive rush to judgment was matched by contempt for the self-serving rush to defense.

This exchange has been dignified by a powerful dose of what people used to call argument ad hominem. In his open letter to Jon Wiener, J. Hillis Miller characterized the "violence" of the denunciation of de Man and of deconstruction as

> a reaction to the genuine threat posed by de Man's work and by that of the so-called deconstructionists generally to a powerful tradition of ideological assumptions about literature, about history, and about the relation of literature to human life. Fear of this power in "deconstruction" and in contemporary theory generally, in all its diversity, accounts better than any other explanation for the unreasoning hostility, the abandoning of the canons of

journalistic and academic responsibility, in articles like yours and the many other subsequent attacks on de Man, on "deconstruction," and on critical theory as such.[15]

Operating from the opposite side of the politico-cultural barricade, Roger Kimball characterized Geoffrey Hartman's troubled essay in the March 7, 1988, issue of the *New Republic* as an early contribution to a massive campaign of "damage control":

> That this paragon [de Man] of chic academic achievement should stand revealed as the author of anti-Semitic articles for pro-Nazi publications at the height of Hitler's power has been a major embarrassment for his many epigones. The reason is obvious: the frequently heard charge that deconstruction is essentially nihilistic has now acquired existential support of the most damaging kind. . . . It is clear that whatever remorse or chagrin Professor de Man's admirers experienced has been completely overshadowed by a concerted effort at creative exculpation—that is to say, at damage control.[16]

This sort of rhetoric constitutes one version of what is currently called historicity. That is, the antagonists are, in the words of the historian Joan Scott, emphasizing "the relevance of the position or situatedness of subjects to the knowledge they produce and the effects of the difference on knowledge."[17] Or, to be exact, the situatedness of the other fellow. In this debate, people historicize each other with a vengeance. I cling to the old-fashioned notion that even if both parties have correctly described their antagonists' (conscious or unconscious) motives, I have yet to hear convincing arguments about the factual content or the moral implications of de Man's behavior from 1940 to 1942. Which is to say that there is something to the genetic fallacy.[18]

Those who objected to the "irresponsible" exploitation of the scandal would not, and could not, confine their polemic to crude or subtle arguments ad hominem. This was not only because the audience they wished to convince would not have been convinced by such arguments but also because they shared an ethic that distinguished bad from good arguments, factual distortions from accurate reconstructions, misrepresentations from responsible descriptions, and lies from truth.

For those who wished to come to grips with what they saw as a biased, vindictive, unfair, irresponsible treatment of what de Man actually did during the Occupation years, there was no choice but to engage in the language of "setting the record straight." These are the very words used in articles and pieces by outstanding figures in the movement labeled deconstruction or postmodernism, and the idea was implied in others. Three of the early contributions to the controversy—by Jonathan Culler, Christopher Norris, and J. Hillis Miller—strikingly illustrate the commitment to conventional standards of accurate reporting, legitimate inference, and respect for fact.

Jonathan Culler, one of the most prolific and influential explicators of postmodernist theory, published a statement in the *Chronicle of Higher Education* for July 13, 1988, entitled "It's Time to Set the Record Straight about Paul de Man and His Wartime Activities for a Pro-Fascist Newspaper." In February 1988, the British scholar Christopher Norris placed a piece in the *London Review of Books* entitled "Paul de Man's Past," in which we again find the statement, "It is important to set the record straight." Those precise words do not appear in J. Hillis Miller's deeply felt essay in the *Times Literary Supplement*, but the essay is vibrant with indignation over the irresponsible handling of facts by those who so readily denigrated de Man: "One would have thought that in a case of such gravity a little checking of facts and rereading of the evidence would have been in order, especially on the part of those journalists who are also professors, professionally committed to a sober truth-telling."[19]

In his one-page piece in the *Chronicle of Higher Education*, Jonathan Culler undertook the task of setting the record straight in language appropriate to a wide audience. The point was to counter the effect of "articles in the press that grossly misrepresent his [de Man's] activities" and whose "innuendos have cast a shadow over his later work."

Culler advances the common-sense argument that de Man's youthful writings did not provide grounds for blanket condemnation of his entire life and works and that his subsequent contributions to literary theory and criticism must be judged on their own merits; then he identifies a connection between de Man's early experience and his later contributions to deconstruction in a repudiation of the "aesthetic ideology"—the key term is "aesthetic"—that informed de Man's early writings. This topic was handled briefly in the *Chronicle* piece but was later afforded a much more detailed analysis by Culler and others, much of it in a dense postmodernist prose not suitable to Culler's mission in the *Chronicle*. The *Chronicle* piece ends with the eminently reasonable conclusion, "The anti-Semitic article and de Man's cooperation with the Nazi occupation are to be condemned. For literary studies, however, the important issue is the value of his subsequent critical work."

In fact, the major part of Culler's short columns is devoted to a mitigation of the condemnation. This is where he goes about setting the record straight. Through his brief outline of the key facts of de Man's collaborationist career, Culler intends to establish that de Man was never a fascist. Culler recounts de Man's participation in *Les Cahiers du libre examen* until the German invasion in 1940; his flight through France to the Spanish border; and his return to Belgium to become a cultural critic for *Le Soir* until "the Nazis reimposed censorship." Culler grants that de Man's articles in *Le Soir* contain too many callow judgments, express a certain optimism regarding a new Europe under German hegemony, and praise German energy and the German cultural tradition, "but not Hitler, not the Nazi party, not the German government or its policies. However dismaying their sentiments in the light of what later occurred, the articles were not pro-Nazi." Furthermore, there is evidence that de Man helped to publish books containing work by writers of the Resistance, and he was cleared by the military prosecutor's office in 1945, at a time when liberated Belgium was treating collaborationists with great severity.

There remains the painful problem of "the one dismaying column"—that is, "The Jews in Contemporary Literature," written in a special anti-Semitic section of *Le Soir*. Perhaps, Culler conjectures, this was stupidly written by de Man to please his employers, but other articles bear no trace of such views. Indeed, one article praises Charles Péguy, who was one of the heroes of the Dreyfus case and therefore the antithesis of an anti-Semite. And there was the testimony of Jews who knew de Man during the Occupation and did not believe that he was an anti-Semite.

In this brief space Culler laid out themes that would be repeated and elaborated elsewhere after all the pieces de Man published between 1940 and 1943 became available. The essential thrust of this history was to rectify the moral balance sheet of de Man's collaborationism through an appeal to one version of objectivity: eliciting all of the relevant facts before rushing to judgment.

Culler's subsequent contributions to the debate briefly cover the same ground, qualifying any categorical condemnation of de Man's behavior during the war. Culler contributed one of the six responses to Derrida's original essay in *Critical Inquiry*, where in contrast to the other responders he gently criticized Derrida's "exceedingly severe statement" to the effect that de Man's writings taken altogether conformed to the rhetoric of the Occupation forces.[20]

Christopher Norris first "set the record straight" in the February 1988 issue of the *London Review of Books*, where he was more concerned with misconstructions of deconstructionism and de Man's contribution to it than with the wartime writings. He did concede that he had no wish "to minimize the

disturbing impact" of those de Man pieces that could be read as an endorsement of the collaborationist line, and "such mystified ideas as the organic
relation between language, culture, and national destiny," especially where
German writers, artists, and intellectuals are praised as having most authen-
tically expressed the sense of cultural nationhood. "But"—there is always a
but—there are points to be made "against the current course of blame."
Articles that had been mined to show de Man in the worst light were alien to
anything that he subsequently wrote, and there were the intense pressures of
political and personal circumstance. Like his Uncle Hendrik, Paul was search-
ing for some way forward through the appalling reality, perhaps through the
acceptance of German hegemony. In his response to critics of this piece in the
letter columns of the *London Review of Books*,[21] Norris strikes what have become familiar notes, balancing the deplorable nature of some of de Man's
articles off against their "deep ambivalence," citing his praise of Péguy, his
positive reference to Kafka, and his sympathy with the Surrealists and writers
linked to the French Resistance—and all of this under "the very real threat of
reprisals from the Nazi censorship."

The postscript that Norris added to his subsequent book on Paul de Man in
order to bring it up to date on the wartime writings repeated these arguments
in a somewhat more elaborate form.[22] Norris first assumed the critical posture
that "it is hard, if not impossible, to redeem these texts by looking for some
occasional sign that they are not to be taken at face value"; then, if not
precisely attempting to "redeem" the offending texts, he did manage to tease
out "hints of a different reading" of passages that seem to affirm German
hegemony and superiority over France and in general celebrate the German
tradition, cultural values, and literature. Norris even conjectures that de Man
"hadn't so completely abandoned those values of liberal, enlightened critique"
that he had espoused before the war.

In a *TLS* column and in a bitterly hostile open letter to Jon Wiener, his
colleague at the University of California, Irvine, J. Hillis Miller set about setting
the record straight, not with those very words but with a greater emotional
intensity than Culler or Norris.[23] Miller was outraged by the "extraordinary
falsifications, misreadings, distortions and selective slanting of quotations,
both of what de Man actually said in those writings and of deconstruction."

With regard to what de Man "actually said," Miller denied that his early writings were totally fascist, anti-Semitic, and collaborationist, and emphasized the
complexity of the facts of the case, including the fact that before the war
de Man participated in a "democratic, anti-clerical, anti-dogmatic, and anti-

fascist" journal. Miller contrasts the postwar clearance of Paul de Man with the condemnation of his uncle, "a prominent Belgian socialist who deluded himself into a brief collaboration with the Germans." Of course there was the "inexcusable, unforgettable" anti-Semitic article in *Le Soir*, Miller acknowledged, and "one sentence echoing anti-Semitic rhetoric" in *Het Vlaamsche Land*. De Man's use of anti-Semitic language to claim that the Jews had not corrupted European culture was deplorable, but not the equivalent of saying that the Jews were a pollution to western Europe. More categorically, in his open letter to Wiener, Miller asserted that "de Man unequivocally condemns what he calls 'vulgar anti-Semitism' and vigorously criticizes the 'myth' of a Jewish 'pollution' of European literature." De Man's condemnation of vulgar anti-Semitism and his reference to Kafka as an exemplary modern author are possibly examples of "the kind of double-talk one learns to practice under totalitarian regimes." None of this exonerates the man, Miller grants, from whatever support his essay might have given to the murderous policies of the occupiers, but it was not straight party-line anti-Semitism of the sort expressed in the adjacent articles in that edition of *Le Soir*. De Man did review the books of various French collaborationists, but in a more or less critical manner; his Belgian coevals who knew him testified that he was neither a collaborationist nor an anti-Semite. Miller also conjectures that de Man wrote the "stupid and deplorable" article on the Jews to please his employers and keep his job, but then goes on to cite de Man's letter to the Harvard authorities asserting that he left *Le Soir* when Nazi censorship made it impossible for him any longer to express himself freely. This juxtaposition deserves comment, which it will receive below.

It was after I had been struck by the dedication to conventional criteria of valid historical discourse in the writings of these three distinguished scholars that I came upon the citation of all three in a paragraph by Pauline Marie Rosenau in a work on postmodernism in the social sciences:

> Some skeptical post-modernists, perhaps exaggerating to create an effect, charge that every interpretation is false (Miller, 1981:249); every understanding is misunderstanding (Culler, 1982:176). "Every reading of a text will always be to some extent a misreading, a version that selects certain details, meaning or structural features at the expense of other details which could just as well have figured in the critic's account" (Norris, 1988:129). What is actually written is not so important because a text (any event) does not constrain interpretation; interpretation, rather, models the text.[24]

The apparent discrepancy between the radical skepticism of the deconstructionist luminaries and their ad hoc insistence on rigorous evidential standards has provided considerable ammunition for their critics, who accuse them of a rhetorical double standard by which "the theorist feels free to exempt himself from his own strictures."[25]

This is an issue that I will pursue not so much to identify abstract philosophic contradictions but to consider the choice of the grounds for convincing argument in the particular circumstances of the de Man case. Those concerned with setting the record straight had no choice but to appeal to conventional criteria of veridicality. To the extent that they affirmed such standards, they joined a certain community—one that is conceptually and ethically committed to "an adequate reading of the facts of the case," as J. Hillis Miller put it.

Now, there is an immense literature to remind us that "an adequate reading of the facts" is no simple task, not even with regard to such a "grossly palpable fact"[26] as de Man's having published in the German-controlled Belgian press from December 1940 until March 1943. The ambivalence about the autonomy of "hard facts" has long haunted the history profession. In contemporary discourse intended to undermine any "privileged" claims to objectivity, foundationalism, or representationalism, the assertion of the authority of some fact external to the observer is worse than suspect.

Yet no such skepticism was summoned to historicize Ortwin de Graef's "discovery." No one chose to deconstruct his privileging of certain methods of historical investigation. No one questioned "the assumption that facts somehow speak for themselves, unaffected by the way knowledge-production is organized."[27] No one suggested that de Graef engage in a self-reflexive analysis of his personal and conceptual *Weltanschauung*. What he had uncovered was simply accepted as a valid representation of past behavior documented according to familiar conventions. Other evidence regarding past events was also treated as unproblematic. For example, testimony by Jewish friends of de Man that he had sheltered them at some personal risk when they were locked out of their apartment was simply taken on its face as a description of what had actually happened.

This deference to the authority of historical documentation was shared by the antagonists in the widening debate. The sharing is what made the debate possible. This is not to say that the conflict might have been settled by superior documentation. That conflicting conclusions were drawn from the same evidence might seem to support the currently influential view that historical narratives are essentially incommensurable, that they cannot simply be reduced to the sum of their "propositional assertions."[28] Variously plotted narratives do, however, often overlap, not only (as in this case) with regard to what constitutes relevant evidence but also with regard to what matters in constituting the narrative and what counts toward establishing the argument embedded in it. Indeed, some such overlapping is necessary for there to be an intelligible historical controversy.

Even though radically different histories of de Man—stories of his life— were fashioned out of the knowledge of his wartime behavior, they proceeded from the common assumption that such a narrative had been irreversibly transformed in the light of new evidence, and from a common identification of the moral and rational grounds for debating the implications of the evidence. The debate depended, for example, on the assumption (still not universally shared) that writing for a collaborationist journal was prima facie deplorable. As for rational grounds, the implicit consensus on what matters and what counts is what allows Culler and others to write in the language of setting the record straight.

The extent to which they succeeded in their campaign remains disputable, partly because there was considerably more to the record than Culler and the others had realized when they undertook to set it straight. Christopher Norris charged the "current chorus of blame" with mining articles "that show him [de Man] in the worst possible light,"[29] but that seemed an appropriate response to the insistence that any judgment of de Man be founded on his entire wartime oeuvre. However, as Norris was aware by the time he appended the postscript to his book on de Man, reference to innocuous passages could not simply cancel out the damaging passages to which he and other defenders of de Man were to devote the most meticulous sympathetic scrutiny.

From the beginning, the most vulnerable essay—not only an embarrassment but the source of personal pain to de Man's Jewish friends and students— was "Les Juifs dans la littérature actuelle" (see Appendix B), which was framed by articles far uglier than his in an issue of *Le Soir* introduced by the paper's proud affirmation of an anti-Semitism that was not merely social but racial— "Notre antisémitisme est d'ordre racial."[30]

De Man's essay deplores a "vulgar anti-Semitism" that condemns European literature as degenerate and decadent because Judaized. The Jews themselves have contributed to the myth of Jewish dominance, interpreted as one of the disastrous consequences of the First World War. But literature has been healthier than that, because it followed its own logic, especially in the psychological realism practiced by such exemplars as Gide, Kafka, Hemingway, and

Lawrence (much will be made of this incongruous list). Jews have had relatively little influence on this development, despite their cerebral qualities, which might have been appropriate to the work of lucid analysis that novels require. In France, for example, Jewish writers have always been of the second rank. (Here de Man presents a list beginning with André Maurois and ending with Julian Benda from which the name of Marcel Proust is notable by its absence.) This phenomenon should comfort Western intellectuals, whose civilization has demonstrated its health through preserving its original character, "despite Semitic interference in all aspects of European life."

This article concludes with the notorious passage luridly illuminated by the hindsight that de Man could not have possessed in 1941: "What's more, one can thus see that a solution to the Jewish problem that would lead to the creation of a Jewish colony isolated from Europe would not have regrettable consequences for the literary life of the West. It would lose, in all, some personalities of mediocre worth and would continue, as in the past, to develop according to its higher laws of evolution."

The assumption that this piece contained the only reference to Jews turned out to be incorrect. In a survey of contemporary German fiction in *Het Vlaamsche Land*, August 20, 1942, de Man contrasts two forms of postwar literary composition that were materially separated by the events of 1933:

> The first of these groups celebrates an art with a strongly cerebral disposition, founded upon some abstract principles and very remote from all naturalness. The theses of expressionism, though very remarkable in themselves, were used here as tricks, as skillful artifices aimed at easy effects. The very legitimate basic rule of artistic transformation, inspired by the personal vision of the creator, served here as a pretext for a forced, caricatured representation of reality. Thus [the artists of this group] came into an open conflict with the proper tradition of German art which had always and before everything else clung to a deep spiritual sincerity. Small wonder, then, that it was mainly non-Germans, and specifically Jews, who went in this direction.[31]

Admittedly, this is a passing reference, but read in the light of the earlier article, it constitutes a further representation of the Jew as an alien element in European culture. Along with this fragmentary but extremely damaging evidence of de Man's acquiescence in the politico-cultural agenda of the controlled press, there was a great deal of other material in book reviews and comments on the cultural scene that could not be dismissed as politically innocuous.

Various reviews and essays contained passages asserting the acceptance of German hegemony as a historical necessity, affirming a certain cultural nationalism with a racialist coloring, praising the accomplishments of Italian fascism, comparing French culture and politics unfavorably to German, and urging collaboration with the conqueror as simple realism. Against this damaging dossier, those committed to a "balanced" judgment could cite pieces that cut against the fascist grain: praising Surrealism, repudiating the total subordination of art to politics, and recommending the French journal *Messages*, a highly suspect publication in the eyes of Belgian and French fascist ideologues.

But these citations did not seem sufficient to balance off the most offensive passages, especially those featured in a series of reviews of Belgian, German, and French authors remembered for their collaborationist or even fascist sympathies. The reviews of French authors constitute a list of what Jeffrey Mehlman called the "Nazi hit parade"[32]—Robert Brasillach, Pierre Drieu La Rochelle, Jacques Chardonne, Marcel Jouhandeau, Albert Fabre-Luce, Bertrand de Jouvenel, and Jacques Benoist-Méchin, most of whom were on the *Gesamtliste des foerdernswerten Schrifttums*, the list of "publications worthy of support" compiled by the Wehrmacht's Propaganda Abteilung in France.

Such reviews constitute a cumulatively damning dossier of de Man's contribution to the German propaganda campaign in Belgium. This was apparent to his defenders, who responded to the serial citation of selected documents with the insistence that each of the apparently deplorable essays deserved a meticulous second reading. Furthermore, the individual texts taken all together could only be understood and judged in historical context—in relation to the very circumstances under which they were written. As this conviction dawned, Jacques Derrida was summoned to the lists.

Derrida answered the summons in a sixty-two-page essay in *Critical Inquiry*[33] that would provide a dialectically ingenious reading designed to draw the sting from the criticism of de Man's most vulnerable articles. It was still possible in mid-1988 to read the controversy as a "struggle for cultural authority" between academic theorists and journalists,[34] but the locus of the debate would shift from newspapers and upper-middle-brow journals to the organs of the academy. The benchmark of this transition was Derrida's essay, which would come to serve as a model or a target for subsequent commentators, depending on the commentator's *parti pris*. For Christopher Norris it was a "fine and compassionate essay"; according to Walter Kendrick, it came swathed in "vintage Derridean fogbanks."[35] Other critics would remark an uncharacteristic lucidity and an assertion of determinable meanings and inferential standards rather alien to Derrida's usual rhetoric.[36]

Whatever its consistency with the expository principles of Derrida's other writings, the essay on de Man certainly does appeal to conventional criteria of responsible argument, those standards of "caution, rigor, honesty" violated by newspaper journalism and by "certain academics." These were the standards that should ground any reading of de Man's wartime writings and any description of his wartime experience: "The reconstitution and the analysis of what his experience was of that war and that occupation will require patient, careful, minute, and difficult research. Any conclusion that does not rely on such research would be unjust, abusive, and irresponsible."[37]

To the extent that Derrida was engaged in the refutation of those who have violated the standards of rigor and honesty, he fashioned a language appropriate to the task. He not only privileged (as postmodernists like to say) conventional criteria of veridicality—the publicly accessible text that constrains interpretation, if it does not impose legitimate readings; the drawing of plausible inference from relevant evidence; the rules of logical coherence—but also borrowed the authority of the appurtenances of conventional historical scholarship, including footnotes. One of these, a two-page depiction of Paul's famous uncle, emphasizes his rapid disenchantment with the Germans and conveys the impression of a temporary aberration within an exemplary career.[38]

To be sure, Derrida does not completely depend on the authority of dispassionate argument and scholarly paraphernalia. The pervasive use of the first-person singular carries the claim to a different sort of authority—the authority of moral indignation at the "newspaper war," and the authority of the pathos of personal implication, of the pain of reading a friend's text that first inflicted "a wound, a stupor, and the sadness that I would neither dissimulate or exhibit."[39]

One might accept the evident sincerity of the self-revelation and the pathos while noting their polemical function—that is, to contribute an emotional authenticity to Derrida's central argument, which grants the deplorable implications of de Man's most shocking texts in order to legitimate a mitigating reading of them. This strategy is embodied in a dichotomous presentation: "on the one hand—evidence as to de Man's serving the German rulers by writing for a paper under their control," and "on the other hand," the material conceivably containing ambiguity, irony, and double meaning, allowing an interpretation that suggests not merely considerable qualification of his Nazi or Fascist or even pro-German sympathies, but doubt about his having been a collaborationist at all. Derrida's interpretation has been characterized favorably or unfavorably as applying techniques of deconstruction to the most damaging of the twenty-five texts then available to him; but if deconstruction is understood to undermine the confidence in the relevance of authorial identity, or the authoritative interpretation of a particular text, this is not what Derrida does. Despite the fact that he poses the possibility of a dichotomous reading, we are left not with a multiplicity of valid/invalid interpretations but with a conclusion: "He [de Man] was aware of having never collaborated or called for collaboration with a Nazism that he never even named in his texts."[40] This is Derrida's conclusion, despite the powerful concession of the preliminary "on the one hand":

> *On the one hand*, the *massive, immediate, and dominant* effect of all these texts is that of a *relatively* coherent ideological ensemble which, *most often and in a preponderant fashion*, conforms to the official rhetoric, that of the occupation forces or of the milieu that, in Belgium, had accepted defeat and, if not state and governmental collaboration as in France, then at least the prospective of a European unity under German hegemony [emphasis in original].[41]

This is a strong statement. Indeed, it is a much more critical reading of the consequences of de Man's journalism than are the interpretations of many who have followed Derrida in teasing out the mitigating elements in the most offensive articles. In a subsequent response to his critics,[42] Derrida insisted that a careful reading prohibits any objection to his "on the other hand," which identifies the ambiguities, the contrary emphases, "a double edge and a double bind" that he interpreted as nonconformist and even ultimately subversive allusions beneath the hard carapace of German censorship.

To balance off his own devastating "on the one hand" and to dispose of the simple assumption that to write for an organ controlled by the Propaganda Abteilung was prima facie collaborationist, Derrida engages in a close reading of the most vulnerable texts to infer a plausible qualifying interpretation. This might be considered the point at which a sensitive hermeneutics is summoned to counterbalance the literal-minded epistemology of a first reading, but Derrida actually casts his argument in the language of social science when he poses the dichotomy as a "hypothesis" tested by an examination of three texts that seem on the surface to serve the masters of the Belgian press.

The salient instance of Derrida's experimental method is his rereading of the notorious piece "Les Juifs dans la littérature actuelle."[43] Having said "on the one hand" that "nothing . . . will heal over the wound I right away felt" when first reading the anti-Semitic passages, which seemed "in the *dominant* context in which they were read in 1941" to produce a dominant effect "in the direction of the worst," Derrida provides a close reading in support of his "on the other hand," suggesting that de Man subtly contrived to undermine his ostensible message.

The key to Derrida's countervailing interpretation is the hypothesis that de Man's dismissal of "vulgar anti-Semitism" might be read as implicitly condemning anti-Semitism *tout court*, inasmuch as anti-Semitism is "always and essentially vulgar":

> What does this article say? It is indeed a matter of criticizing vulgar anti-semitism. That is the primary, declared, and underscored intention. But to scoff at vulgar antisemitism, is that also to scoff at or mock the vulgarity of antisemitism? This latter syntactic modulation leaves the door open to two interpretations. To condemn vulgar antisemitism may leave one to understand that there is a distinguished antisemitism in whose name the vulgar variety is put down. De Man never says such a thing, even though one may condemn his silence. But the phrase can also mean something else, and this reading can always contaminate the other in a clandestine fashion: to condemn "vulgar antisemitism," *especially if one makes no mention of the other kind*, is to condemn antisemitism itself *inasmuch as* it is vulgar, always and essentially vulgar. De Man does not say that either. If that is what he thought, a possibility I will never exclude, he could not say so clearly in this context. One will say at this point: his fault was to have accepted the context. Certainly, but what is that, to accept a context? and what would one say if he claimed not to have fully accepted it, and to have preferred to play the rule there of the nonconforming smuggler, as so many others did in so many different ways, in France and in Belgium, at this or at that moment, inside or outside the Resistance? [emphasis in original]

Critics of Derrida's essay subsequently observed that his hypothesis immediately hardens to the flat description of the article as "non-conformist, as Paul de Man, as also his uncle, always was." Then, categorically, "it is a matter of condemning antisemitism *inasmuch as it is vulgar*." The other brutally anti-Semitic articles on the same page support the hypothesis, because even if de Man's article is "contaminated by the forms of vulgar anti-Semitism that frame it, *these coincide in a literal fashion, in their vocabulary and logic, with the very thing that de Man accuses*, as if his article were denouncing the neighboring articles."

After establishing his interpretation of the remarks on "vulgar antisemitism" as an Aesopian critique of *Le Soir*'s anti-Semitic program, Derrida reads the central body of the article as having no relation to the Jewish question, merely speaking to literature, so that what remains is the last section, "and the only one that can be suspected of antisemitism." There he must deal with the "paragraph that remains for me disastrous"—de Man's evocation of a Europe without Jews. This passage leaves "an indelible wound" but does not impose "a general judgment, with no possibility of appeal." There are still questions to be posed. For example, de Man refers positively to the Jewish writer Kafka, and in another article he praises Péguy the Dreyfusard. And who can say under what circumstances the text was published? Of course de Man could have left the paper, "but [here Derrida transforms his conjecture into a categorical opinion] he would have had to be certain that this rupture was a better idea than his ambiguous and sometimes anti-conformist continuation on the job." That final allusion to "a Jewish colony isolated from Europe" remains, in the light of the present state of information, impossible to understand. Perhaps de Man was thinking of the so-called Madagascar solution; at that date he would certainly not have been thinking of the Final Solution, which had not yet been put into effect.

Derrida's disposition of "Les Juifs dans la littérature actuelle" functions as an argument a fortiori. If the article on the Jews, perceived as the worst case, isn't as bad as it seems, the lesser offenses are diminished. Hereafter, Derrida applies the working principle—that all of de Man's "propositions carry within them a counter-proposition"—to other salient texts, to the same effect.

One more example of the dialectical dexterity with which Derrida defused a few of the most damaging texts is his reading of de Man's review of Jacques Chardonne's book *Voir la Figure*. Chardonne was a leading Nazi sympathizer and the spokesman for the hard-core French collaborationists who gathered in Weimar in 1941 to rally the support of intellectuals for the German war effort. Praising Chardonne's clear-headed reflections on German reality (*le fait allemand*), de Man wrote,

This war will only bring a tighter union between things that were so close from the start—the Hitlerian soul and the German soul—to the point that they will become a single and unique power. This is an important phenomenon because it means that one cannot judge the fact of Hitler without at the same time judging the fact of Germany and that the future of Europe can be envisioned only in the framework of the possibilities and the needs of the German spirit. It is not only a matter of a series of reforms, but of the definitive emancipation of a people that finds itself, in its turn, called upon to exercise hegemony in Europe.[44]

De Man grants that the fascinating possibilities of this future are not exempt from dangerous temptations, but he concludes, "It is a merit of a work such as that of Chardonne, to be able to raise itself sufficiently above the melee to cast a glance outward toward the horizons that draw closer each day."

Derrida presents this as an example of de Man's "clever and not very docile strategy," through an ingenious explication of the last sentence of de Man's first paragraph, which reads, "Après de telles phrases, on pourra peut-être discuter les idées de Chardonne mais certes pas leur reprocher de manquer de netteté." The thrust of the entire passage inclines one to translate that last clause, "One can perhaps differ with Chardonne's ideas but certainly not reproach them for lack of clarity." Derrida chooses another meaning of *netteté*, giving us "reproach them for lack of sharpness." Thus, he suggests that this is "a double-edged sentence—on sharpness, precisely, and on the cutting edge itself. One may suppose, without being sure, that de Man judges these ideas to be very debatable."[45]

Thus de Man anticipates Derrida's conceit of the "double-cut" and subtly undermines the plain sense of his favorable review. Such an example of how to be the master rather than the servant of words provided a precedent for the way that de Man's defenders might balance the scales.

However one assays the balance of Derrida's judgment on de Man's wartime behavior, it is apparent that Derrida identifies some contemporary behavior as far worse than what de Man did under the pressures of historical circumstance. "To judge, to condemn the work or the man on the basis of what was a brief episode, to call for closing, that is to say, at least figuratively, for censoring or burning his books is to reproduce the exterminating gesture which one accuses de Man of not having armed himself against sooner with the necessary vigilance. It is not even to draw a lesson that he, de Man, learned to draw from the war."[46]

What Derrida first presented more or less tentatively, his successors in *Responses* and elsewhere argued categorically. Using Derrida's framing technique, other defenders of de Man and deconstruction played off a milder "on the one hand" against a more conclusive "on the other." Thus the reading of de Man's most embarrassing text—on the Jews and literature as essentially Aesopian—has become the canonical reading.

Thomas Fries concluded that while (on the one hand) the "apparently minimal effects of these inflammatory articles cannot excuse them in any way," de Man "overestimated his ability to outwit the Germans and greatly underestimated the gravity of the context. Those who do not take into consideration this hypothesis misjudge the real power relations and the resulting constraints upon writing (equivocalness as weapon)."[47] For Ian Balfour, de Man's essay is (on the one hand) "an outrageous article with a deeply disturbing conclusion," but (on the other), "the contradictory impulses in the article—the hypothesis of the Europe free of Jewish writers together with an attack on vulgar anti-Semitism and a canonization of Kafka suggest a scene of writing . . . of philosophical texts written under political pressure."[48] Peggy Kamuf defends the interpretation of de Man's equivocal contributions as "a form of contraband smuggling" through a challenge to "categorical refutation": "Nothing learned so far about the circumstances of de Man's association with *Le Soir*, and nothing one can read in these articles, exclude that the young man made some calculation and accepted to *impose* an ideological cover on his journalistic exercise, that he accepted, as again Derrida puts it, to grasp the 'double edge' placed in his hands."[49]

Such an approach was applied to other potentially reprehensible articles in *Le Soir* and *Het Vlaamsche Land*. With the republication of all of de Man's contributions to these journals, as well as the reviews and book notes for the *Bibliographie Dechenne*, considerably more palliative "on the other hands" would be required to draw the sting from so many "on the one hands." This task was shouldered in a most thorough and literal-minded manner by Ortwin de Graef, almost as if to expiate his sin in opening the cover of the tomb.[50] De Graef scrupulously uncovers various apparently collaborationist pieces, while finding a reason to suggest in each case that "matters are certainly not as simple as they might appear at first sight." A second reading, De Graef argues, suggests that de Man "never uncritically praises any of the collaborationist books he reviews, but characteristically preserves a tellingly indeterminate margin of disagreement." De Graef thus considers some twelve examples that seem to express collaborationist and pro-German sentiment, including the two anti-Semitic passages, all accompanied by a mitigating gloss. The very length of the list suggests the problem of serial exculpation, and this is not an exhaustive list.

After sufficient communion with this style of argument, one begins to get the hang of it, as I hope I am about to demonstrate.

In a brief book note published in the *Bibliographie Dechenne* in September 1942, cited by Alice Yaeger Kaplan and David Carroll[51] but to my knowledge mentioned by none of de Man's defenders, de Man reviewed Lucien Rebatet's *Les Décombres*, a French best-seller in 1942 and 1943. Rebatet was a French fascist, without apology or qualifications, whose condemnation to death at the end of the war was commuted because sufficient time had passed to render the death penalty unpopular. *Les Décombres*—"the ruins," or "the rubbish"—was a diatribe against all of the mistakes and blunders that led to the catastrophic decline of France, and an affirmation of the virtues of fascism. It was the vehicle of a vicious anti-Semitism ornamented by such passages as this: "After one hundred and fifty years of Jewish emancipation, these evil impure beasts carrying within themselves the germs of every plague ought to be returned to the prisons where the secular wisdom had once incarcerated them."[52] Here is what de Man had to say about the book:

> Lucien Rebatet, like Robert Brasillach, is one of those young French intel-lectuals who, during the years between the two [world] wars, worked with all their might to combat a politics whose catastrophic and ill-fated orientation they had understood. The entire sum of bitterness and indignation accumu-lated over the course of those years of vain combat finally overflows [*dé-borde*] in this thick volume, an immense pamphlet of brilliant verve and vigor. One by one, all the guilty parties of the current French decay, what-ever the milieu or party to which they belong, are looked over and shot down in a few lapidary and definitive sentences. But this great work of destruction also contains constructive elements: in walking among the ruins [*les décombres*] of a bankrupt era, Lucien Rebatet also dreams of reconstruc-tion; and this is why without a doubt his ferocious book ends in words of hope.

"Rebatet's hope," remarks David Carroll, "is for a fascist Europe domi-nated by a Nazi Germany in which France, having itself become fascist, would play a major role." On the Derrida model, the approved way to handle this hot potato might go something like this:

> On first reading, this seems to be a recommendation to the Belgian reading public of an unequivocally profascist and viciously anti-Semitic work. Noth-ing can excuse that, above all in the light of consequences not foreseen by de Man, but it is not enough to stop with condemnation, which would be to speak the language of the totalitarian spirit voiced by Rebatet. One should

allow at least the possibility of an, unverifiable but necessary, alternate reading. As obnoxious as it is, Rebatet's obscene text does not recommend the extermination of the Jews but only their incarceration in a worldwide network of ghettos. Furthermore, to recommend the work, or apparently to recommend the work, is not necessarily to commend it. De Man is simply describing it, and in language that is not unambiguously positive. Here the key word is overflow (*déborde*)—an overflow obviously refers to an excess. That is to say that there is something excessive about Rebatet's work against which, in his subtly defiant manner, de Man is warning the readers. We know that de Man believes that this is a ferocious book. He hasn't said that he shares its words of hope. Furthermore, what effect could the review have had? It's hard to believe that Belgians in this period of dearth ran out to spend their francs on a book just because a young reviewer recommended it.

And so forth, with special emphasis on the incipient totalitarianism of those who would condemn, without qualification, de Man's blurb for a very nasty piece of work.

This rhetoric of partial admission, followed by a tentative mitigation that hardens into categorical exculpation, has the flavor of plea-bargaining by the hard-pressed attorney for the defense. Perhaps this is inevitable. As Dennis Donoghue remarked, "It would be agreeable if someone could propose any alternative to the idiom of prosecution and defense, but I can't see how this is possible."[53] In fact, it seemed impossible for those who objected to any sort of posthumous trial of de Man to eschew legalistic language.

Having objected to the prosecutorial stance of John Brenkman's contribution to *Responses* or to a posthumous trial of de Man, Geoffrey Hartman proceeded to appeal to the principle of "reasonable doubt" and the spirit of the First Amendment:

> To condemn the articles on the basis of their ideas would mean we had clarified what was called *délit d'opinion* in the French purges after Liberation. In a democracy we do not prosecute ideas as such. Proof is required that they directly incited criminal or treasonous activities. Despite Brenkman's effort, I do not think we have that proof. The essays stick to cultural issues and do not support particular measures of the occupier or denounce individuals or groups.[54]

Since there is no proof that de Man denounced individuals or groups, he deserves the benefit of the doubt. And so too, presumably, does every other writer who affirmed the realism of collaboration, identified the Hitlerian soul with the German soul and praised the works of fascist authors, but who brought no one in particular to the attention of the Gestapo.

There is an even more radical disjuncture between Jacques Derrida's disclaimers and his line of argument.

> I have said why I am not speaking here as a judge, witness, prosecutor, or defender in some trial of *Paul de Man*. One will say: but you are constantly delivering judgment, you are evaluating, you did so just now. Indeed, and therefore I did not say that I would not do so at all. I said that in analyzing, judging, evaluating this or that discourse, this or that effect of these old fragments, I refuse to expand these gestures to a general judgment, with no possibility of appeal, of Paul de Man, of the totality of what he was, thought, wrote, taught, and so forth.

Apparently the repudiation of the general judgment with no possibility of appeal still licenses Derrida to appeal to the "unquestionable fact" that

> a statement can never be taken as a presumption of guilt or evidence in a trial, even less as proof, as long as one has not demonstrated that it has only an idiomatic value and that no one else, besides Paul de Man or of Paul de Man's signatory of the 1940–42 texts, could have either produced this statement or subscribed to it. Or inversely, that all statements—their numbers are not finite and their contexts are highly diverse—could not be signed and approved by authors who shared nothing of Paul de Man's history or political experiences.

Having entered this ingenious demurrer, Derrida gives up "this petty and mediocre game," a technique he applies in various places to disavow inappropriate arguments that he has just made. Thus he disclaims any appeal to his own background, which might authenticate his arguments in favor of de Man, remarking that he was Jewish, persecuted during the war, known for his leftist opinions, and so forth, but then assuring the reader that "such declarations are insufficient."[55]

The technique of ritual disclaimer followed by arguments designed to undo it is a recurrent tactic for all of those who begin by saying that what de Man did was inexcusable and then go on to excuse what he did. This approach is fortified by the evidential double standard. As Marjorie Perloff observes, not all statements of witnesses who speak well of de Man are subject to the stringent scrutiny applied to the damaging evidence. When this technique is applied directly to the texts, "positive readings are cognitive, negative ones are merely judgmental and moralistic."[56]

The most convincing argument in de Man's defense depending on reference to historical fact speaks to the actual context for behavior that it is all too easy to condemn from complacent hindsight. To situate writings in context is a special skill of deconstruction, we are told.[57] If so, it is a skill necessarily cast in the language of setting the record straight, for it assumes that a particular past can be adequately represented (or manifestly misrepresented) and that texts can be illuminated with reference to relevant verifiable circumstance.

Ortwin de Graef situates de Man's writings in the context of the response to the German occupation, which ranged from passive acquiescence to enthusiastic participation in the Nazi New Order. He and other commentators emphasize the difference between de Man's rather ill-advised "Belgicist" nationalism and the self-destructive ultranationalism of Belgian Nazis like Léon Degrelle, which paved the road to Belgium's assimilation in the Third Reich.[58]

The drawing of such distinctions is certainly appropriate in the light of persistent simplifications, as in *The Economist*'s review of Lehman's book, where de Man is simply identified as a Nazi.[59] One can, of course, label any collaborationist a Nazi, but that is poor history, as it blurs the distinctions that contribute to an understanding of the behavior of peoples under the German occupation. A substantial, sophisticated literature on the varieties of French collaborationism has proceeded from these distinctions.[60] We understand very little of the history of Vichy France if we simply identify Pétain's Vichy circle with the Paris Nazis or the numerous, more or less passive *attentistes* with the French Gestapo.

As Zeev Sternhell remarks, many intellectuals and civil servants went further and did far worse than de Man, "but their writings never prevented them from making a great career in the postwar world. . . . In this sense, Jacques Derrida's feeling of injustice in the face of the storm surrounding his dead friend is not entirely unjustified."[61] But it is one thing to say that de Man was not a Nazi and was, indeed, quite a small fry among Belgian collaborationists, and it is another to say that what he did was not all that bad. To make that case requires an appeal to specific extenuating circumstances in the context of daily life in occupied Belgium.

To appeal to context is to criticize those who presume to pass judgment on people who faced inexorable choices that they themselves have never had to confront. In the characteristically pugnacious words of Andrej Warminski, "What do you know about the man, his circumstances, the place, the time? Who are you to draw a line between a good man and a bad man, resistance and collaboration?"[62] This question has considerable force that echoes beyond the circle of de Man's militant defenders, but it resonates differently if directed to his surviving coevals, such as his condisciples at the *Cercle du libre examen* who chose a different path.

There are, however, Belgian contemporaries who do speak in defense of de Man. Edouard Colinet writes, "I am shocked by the attempt to impeach Paul's honor on the part of people who either do not take into account all the facts concerning the period 1940–1944 or have never known them."[63] Colinet speaks with some authority, because he was a friend of de Man, an associate on the board of *Les Cahiers du libre examen*, and a survivor of the Occupation as a member of the French Resistance. Colinet reviews the various activities of the circle of *Les Cahiers*, ranging from heroic resistance to collaborationism, to remind the reader that under the circumstances of the German occupation, the choices with regard to survival were inescapable and extremely difficult and that therefore any "after the fact judgment is easily biased and unfair." Faced with the need to earn a living and support a family, de Man decided to make money in the only way that was open to him: through writing for the German-controlled press. Thus even de Man's anti-Semitic article "written reluctantly" was his response to the need to preserve a livelihood. In some accounts this motive is assumed as a justification for whatever de Man did. According to Ernesto Laclau, "all witnesses agree" that de Man's publication in *Le Soir* "was no act of ideological identification, but resulted entirely from his need to ensure a livelihood for his family."[64]

Jean Stengers, a historian and an expert on the Belgian Right, also emphasizes de Man's need to make a living: "most Belgians who did things like that, even if they sometimes met with strong disapproval, were after a while easily pardoned." Stengers also disposes of the essay on the Jews with reference to the context of Belgian opinion at the time. That is, while the Jews had already been expelled from public office, "the time of their real ordeal had not yet begun. So there was not yet any particular compassion for them among the Belgian non-Jewish people. At the time of the great sufferings and of the great compassion, an article like that of De Man would have been pilloried; but then one may suppose that at that time De Man himself would not have written it." De Graef and Colinet also cite the existence of a certain lack of public sympathy toward the Jews as if this were a mitigating factor.[65]

The absolutely clinching contextual factor, according to de Man's defenders, is the fact that he was not indicted by the Belgian postliberation courts, whose treatment of collaborationists was harsher than that of most of the other countries under German occupation—far harsher than in France.

However, the historical context of de Man's wartime writings—the daily experience of the Occupation in Belgium, the body of writings published under the Nazi aegis, the course of the war and of world events—is precisely what has been emphasized in an intensely critical reaction to the more or less sympathetic reassessments of de Man as collaborationist. Beginning with the responses to Derrida's first article in *Critical Inquiry*, critics of "exculpation through textual reinterpretation" object to the way de Man's defenders read texts as if they could be judged without reference to where and when they appeared and how they were read. From this perspective, "a close reading is completely inappropriate"; all that counts is the "massive effect."[66] "No one," argues David Carroll, "reading this paper [*Le Soir*] or working for it could have any doubts as to where it stood."[67] Thus, contrary to Derrida's reading of "Les Juifs dans la littérature actuelle" as subtly undermining the vicious pieces that framed it, "the anti-Semitic frame totally determines the overall spirit and the tenor; on the page as a whole, de Man's presence (far from counteracting his contributors) graphically exhibits the shame of collaboration, and he is degraded by the company he keeps."[68]

Indeed, those critics who perceive an Aesopian subtext in de Man's wartime writings exhibit a remarkable lack of interest in reader response. Derrida does conjecture that de Man's subtle contradictions of the dominant ideology had to "leave some trace in the consciousness or the unconsciousness of the reader."[69] But whatever the effect in the contemporary unconscious, no one has documented some conscious decoding of the subversive message beneath the collaborationist text.[70]

The most specific justification of de Man's writings in relation to reader response is that they were negligible. They had no effect—therefore, Colinet labels the debate "Much Ado about Nothing." According to Jean Stengers, de Man's activities "found at the time no echo whatsoever." However, in a footnote he does identify one unfortunate echo: the underground pamphlet that includes de Man in a *Galerie des Traitres*.[71]

To postulate an Aesopian subtext as a mitigation of apparently offensive texts is to assume not only an audience that might have decoded it but also a censorship that misread it. While the Propaganda Abteilung did not exercise preventative censorship on the controlled press through most of the period before August 12, 1942, it did control it, laying down the general line at weekly conferences and applying sanctions against journalists who disobeyed instructions.[72] The assumption that the PA censors were more obtuse than our contemporary critics may be valid but scarcely relevant; and the conjecture that they were bamboozled by de Man is dubious, although familiar enough among those intellectuals who believe that they are cleverer than the people they serve. Of course, it is possible that de Man was such an intellectual.

Again, the situation in Belgium can be illuminated with reference to that in France. French writers, like their fellow citizens, ranged from heroic *résistants* to bitter-end collaborationists. It is clear that the latter were not always the most preferred by their masters. As Zeev Sternhell points out,

> The propaganda services in Paris and Brussels did not encourage only vulgar collaboration, which called for people to leave for the eastern front, or to denounce acts of resistance, or to inform on Jews in hiding. The men in charge of German propaganda such as Otto Abetz, Friedrich Grimm, or Karl Epting, had a wonderful knowledge of the mentality of the French-speaking intelligentsia. They grasped that a coarse, low-level anti-Semitism could be counter-productive, and they needed something subtle—something of the kind that one finds, say, in the writings of Henri de Man.[73]

William Flesch pursues the same theme in *Responses*, quoting from the German propaganda specialist Lieutenant Edward Wintermayer to the effect that bridges to French opinion were most effectively built by works arising from "purely French initiatives." This did not require an affirmation of French Nazism—in fact, that was not necessarily desirable. The point was to normalize the situation, to appeal to a realistic acceptance of life under German hegemony. Flesch locates de Man's place in the Belgian spectrum in the light of these observations: his writings served "the occupiers' campaigns to normalize the appearance of the situation."[74]

What might be called the "Otto Abetz alternative" as applied in Belgium is characterized in a postwar Belgian essay on German press policy under the Occupation:

> When the situation was grave, the subjects to be treated, even the titles and sometimes complete articles, were prescribed. As to the rest, an effort was made to maintain the former aspect of the stolen papers. *Vooruit* and *Le Journal de Charleroi* kept a tone of social protest which was supposed to please the readers of the former Socialist papers. *Le Nouveau Journal* bitterly

attacked Flemish separatism which was heralded by *Volk en Staat*. The Germans scarcely bothered to limit these polemics, as long as German interests were not at stake.[75]

This was the regime under which de Man wrote essays that were not always "in conformity with the premises of Nazi politics." As long as de Man's writings, to use Derrida's words, "*most often and in a preponderant fashion*" conformed to official rhetoric, they served the purposes of the Propaganda Abteilung. Whatever his intention, he contributed to the soft sell—to the lowering of "the threshold of acceptability" of the intellectual collaboration.[76]

The concern with context necessarily entails consideration of the actual course of events as the background against which de Man's writings were read. His defenders refer to the chronology of the treatment of Jews in Belgium to establish the fact that he could not have been aware of the Final Solution, even in 1942. The critics, on the other hand, note that the notorious *Le Soir* piece was written after the Germans had imposed registration on the Jews and banned them from the professions, the civil service, and the mass media. De Man's essay referring to the Jews in *Het Vlaamsche Land* on August 20, 1942, appeared after they had been ordered to wear the yellow star and after the first convoy of Jewish deportees had been sent east. Quoting from Raul Hilberg on the general knowledge of the increasingly desperate situation of the Belgian Jews, Sandor Goodhart observes, "In the light of such macabre details, the distinctions between vulgar and non-vulgar anti-semitism begin to sound academic."[77]

The articles proposing a realistic response to irreversible events—that is, acceptance of the occupation—can be read in the context of collaboration and passive acquiescence but also against a background of active and passive refusals to collaborate. Like collaborationism, resistance ranged along a spectrum of behavior: the self-sacrificing heroism that cost the lives of some of de Man's prewar comrades; simple refusals to collaborate—the option exercised by virtually the entire staff of *Le Soir* when it was taken over by the Germans; the painting of V's (for "victory") on city walls; or the avoidance of activities celebrating German-Belgian unity.

The ways of saying no ranged from small individual refusals to collective acts of defiance carried out at varying degrees of risk by combative crowds and respected institutions. The faculty of the *Université Libre de Bruxelles* closed the university rather than accept the imposition of a colleague who had been condemned as a traitor in the First World War. In June 1942 the Bourgmeistres—

municipal officials—refused to implement the imposition of the yellow star. In August 1941, Cardinal van Roey, the Belgian primate, declared, "It is wrong for Catholics to collaborate in the establishment of a tyrannical regime, indeed they are under an obligation to resist such a regime. They must not cooperate with those seeking to establish such a regime in Belgium."[78] De Man's support of collaboration, his remarks on "those still blinded by nationalist passions," were read to the accompaniment of such events. His positive reviews of various events introducing German or Italian culture to the Belgians bear tacit witness to the massive boycott of those activities.

The context of the course of events outside of Belgium also speaks to the nature of de Man's "realism" in assimilating the fact of German hegemony. It is possible that in 1940 de Man, like many others, believed that for the foreseeable future, life would be pursued and culture preserved, if at all, under German domination. This was scarcely the case, however, in 1942. De Man still characterized "the policy of collaboration" as "an irresistible necessity"[79] even after the German army had been thrown back from the gates of Moscow and the United States had entered the war. Perhaps it was possible to believe that Germany might somehow preserve its European hegemony at the end of a protracted struggle. That is, until Stalingrad and the Allied landings in North Africa, after which de Man dropped out, meeting the deadline of the Belgian government-in-exile, which promised to exempt writers from prosecution if they severed relations with the collaborationist press by the end of 1942. From 1943 until the end of the war, de Man and his family survived apparently without a paying job.

The defense of Paul de Man has claimed the epistemological authority of evidence, logic, and context, fortified by an assumption of hermeneutical mastery, implicitly an argument from self-conferred authority couched in the language of a coterie. This tendency is especially evident in the interpretation of the relation between de Man's wartime and postwar writings, where hermeneutics definitely takes over from epistemology and the water begins to close over the reader's head.[80] But the rhetoric of textual analysis, where the identification of figures of speech—catachresis, prolepsis, and so forth—is presumed to be equivalent to refutation of an argument, is also applied to the debate over the wartime writings. Nor do the advocates of setting the record straight completely eschew the polemical uses of indeterminacy, at times to the point of self-parody:

What exactly are we talking about? What does it mean to talk, to ask "about" . . . ? For instance, about the "character" of an individual man? About a practice of language, of reading and rewriting, known as "deconstruction"? About a war fought some half a century ago? About Nazism? Fascism? Collaboration? About academic institutions and academic intellectuals? What about the word "about," that relates the question to its object? To talk "about" something is to position ourselves in its vicinity, to be sure, and yet nevertheless: outside it, alongside perhaps, but still at a certain remove from what we are talking about.[81]

According to Andrej Warminski (who makes quite categorical judgments of critics of de Man, who have, he says, crawled out "from under the rocks of their pathologies"), "Reading suspends: it suspends knowledge and it suspends judgment, and it suspends above all, the possibility of whether we are ever knowing whether we are doing one or the other."[82] Here the key term, the very touchstone, is "reading"—that is, "attentive" reading, in contrast to inattentive reading or not reading at all. Once again, Derrida provides the paradigm. In his diatribe—and that is not too strong a term—against the critics of his first piece in *Critical Inquiry*, the clinching charge is that they *ne pveut pas lire*—fusing *pouvoir* and *vouloir* into a neologism for "they neither can nor wish to read," thus accruing the authority of Derridean wordplay.[83] Derrida's own gloss on de Man's "The Jews in Contemporary Literature" was, according to Rodolphe Gasché, "merely an attentive reading of what this text unmistakably tells us."[84]

In postmodernist discourse, especially in the most admired, mature works of Paul de Man, to read attentively is to emphasize the indeterminacy of texts; but in these condemnations of "self-righteousness at the expense of attentive, sustained reading"[85] or of ignoring "the first and most elementary rule," which is "to read,"[86] it is easy enough to read "attentive" as right and "inattentive" as wrong. Hans-Jost Frey nails this down. Resigned to "the readiness of nonreaders to pass judgment and the refusal of those who would judge to read," he concludes, "Against these judgments one can simply say that, to the extent that they are based on the refusal to read precisely, they are invalid."[87]

One might assume that good readers would have reached a consensus; yet such supremely attentive readers as Geoffrey Hartman and Barbara Johnson, distinguished professors of literature at Yale and Harvard and certainly sympathetic to de Man, regretfully take de Man's essay on the Jews straight up, undiluted by a mitigating subtext—a momentary lapse in attentiveness, perhaps.[88] In fact, the claim to read attentively is a self-authorizing authentication of interpretations, no matter how far removed those interpretations are from the ordinary reader's response to the text. All of this is to beg the question of the validity of particular readings, especially when they strike the unconvinced as "inattentive."

Perhaps the most striking example of collective inattentiveness on the part of those who have urged us to read all of the relevant texts with infinite scruple is the attention paid to the two works that bracket de Man's wartime writings: his contributions to the student press before the German invasion and his 1955 letter to the Harvard Society of Fellows in answer to an anonymous denunciation.

Acknowledging that de Man's essays in *Le Soir* and *Het Vlaamsche Land* did not reflect an awareness of the catastrophic menace of Nazi Germany, Rodolphe Gasché concluded, "But if de Man did not come to grips with the horror that was in the offing, it was *among other things* because his analytical apparatus did not provide the means to capture the viciousness and aberration of the Nazi endeavor *on all fronts*" [emphasis in original].[89]

But de Man's analytical apparatus seemed perfectly adequate to that reality in January 1940. In the November 9, 1939, issue of *Jeudi*, he does defend neutrality, but even there he asserts that Belgium would certainly defend itself if attacked, as it had in 1914. In the piece "Que pensez-vous de la guerre," which appeared in the January 4, 1940, issue of *Jeudi*, de Man articulates the line common to the political Left at that date—that is, categorically anti-Nazi:

> From a strictly anti-imperialist point of view, it would be a grave tactical error to accept an immediate peace, leaving Hitler with immense moral and material gains. One must choose the lesser of two imperialisms, that is to say the English, if only because it is the easier to resist.
>
> In declaring "we must crush Hitlerism" France and England confront the very source of our troubles. But one cannot hope to reach this goal simply through military victory.

De Man then goes on to argue that a true conquest of Hitlerism entailed the transformation of the environment that had made it possible and, in anticipation of the language of the Resistance, envisioned structural reforms that might constitute a "total turnabout" in the domestic and foreign policies of the European states.[90]

Those who assimilate de Man into the prewar West European intelligentsia that was anticapitalist, antiparliamentarian, and quasi-fascist ignore what he was actually writing before the invasion of Belgium. Therefore, Ortwin de Graef's reference to a potentially collaborationist element in prewar Belgium, possibly including Uncle Henri, does not really locate Paul himself—at least not as of January 1940.

In December of that year Paul wrote his first review for *Le Soir*. In the issue of April 12–14, 1941, we read that thanks to the many years of brainwashing (*bourrage de crâne*—the same words Uncle Henri used in his famous manifesto accepting the German Occupation in 1940) of British and French propaganda, the Belgian public knows little of the German social and political accomplishments. This is in a review of various German brochures on the Third Reich, which concludes with reference to a work on the Armistice that compares the conditions imposed in 1918 and 1940: "This study shows how much more honorable, just, and humane was the attitude of the German conquerors than that of the French of 1918 who had in fact achieved a less decisive victory."[91] This radical transformation presents a problem for the interpreters of de Man's wartime writings. To them, de Man's words are seen as an authentic, albeit temporary, philosophic aberration.[92] To his prewar comrades, they were interpreted as turning coat.

The overriding responsibility to read did not especially detain those who cite de Man's 1955 letter to the Harvard Society of Fellows in his favor.[93] Even after the full text of the letter was available, Geoffrey Hartman was able to write, "The ethical situation of de Man differs from that of Heidegger in that there was no retrospective falsification, unless his silence is taken to be that."[94] Whether de Man should be condemned for not having called the equivalent of a press conference to present his mea culpa, or whether his silence about his past was the finest response to it, the fact is that when asked, he lied.

Whatever one makes of his identification of his Uncle Henri as his father, it is a falsehood. And his claim to have left *Le Soir* in 1941 rather than 1942 is not a trivial inaccuracy.[95] All over Europe, there were people resigned to the German occupation through 1941 who were involved in active resistance by the following year. His statement that he wrote some literary articles in *Le Soir* and that "like most of the other contributors, I stopped doing so when Nazi thought control did no longer allow for freedom of statement" is not simply disingenuous but categorically false. The Nazis always exercised thought control over the paper, even when they did not apply preventative censorship. After this was applied on August 20, 1942, de Man contributed fourteen additional articles to *Le Soir*, one more to *Het Vlaamsche Land*, and assorted book notes to the *Bibliographie Dechenne*.

Those who cite in de Man's favor his assertion that he left the paper when the Nazis applied censorship and at the same time conjecture that he must have written the anti-Semitic essay under pressure contradict themselves. These two points are crammed into one paragraph by J. Hillis Miller, who, as Paul Morrison observes, "credits de Man with both a principled decision to quit *Le Soir* when it was no longer possible to 'express himself freely' and with a subversive inclusion of 'double talk' in an article written under compulsion. Clearly both cannot be true, or both can be true only in the context of a 'double talk' that has little to do with the kind one learns to practice under a totalitarian regime."[96]

The cumulative effect on this reader of the apologetic literature has been decidedly negative. While I cannot pretend to an initial neutrality (I once picketed Kirsten Flagstad[97]), I am not alone. Dubious defensive polemics have done more to reinforce a negative perception of what the deconstructionists (or so-called deconstructionists) are about than have all the attempts to establish some sinister linkage between de Man's collaborationism and the post-modernist project. As the historian James Kloppenberg remarks, "Although deconstruction should survive the attack of de Man's critics, as a tool for historians it may not survive de Man's defense."[98] Or, as Paul Morrison puts it, the relevant issue in the debate over de Man's wartime activities was "not what 'resistance to theory' the attack on de Man evinces but what 'resistance to history' the defense of de Man entails."[99] In an essay that argued the conservative political implications of deconstruction, Russell Berman wrote, "The de Man affair brought an end to the deconstructive ascendancy not because the revelations about de Man were so conclusively damning, but because the vacuous responses of his defenders revealed deconstruction's own false bottoms."[100]

The criticism of the cohort that rallied to the standard planted by Miller, Culler, and Derrida is not confined to their antagonists but has also been expressed by those who deplore the weak logic and ignorance of the journalistic denunciations of de Man and deconstruction. Granting the guardians of de Man's reputation every right to be enraged by the intellectual dishonesty and moral irresponsibility of this onslaught, Terry Eagleton identifies something like a self-parody in the rhetoric of de Man's defenders as history, politics, and ethics "emerge from the limbo of indeterminacy with a vengeance." And he awards the "booby prize for special pleading" to a "tortuous, deeply embarrassing contribution from Jacques Derrida."[101]

Louis Menand trenchantly criticized David Lehman's book for its flawed understanding of deconstruction but granted some valid points in Lehman's critique of the apologies for the wartime writings. Quoting some of the deconstructionist apologetics that seemed farfetched and self-serving, Menand points out how the exculpatory interpretations of the wartime writings contradict each other and how they simultaneously attempt to interpret and judge de Man's wartime text while defending "the sufficiency of deconstruction as critical practice."[102]

Dominick LaCapra, a historian open to postmodernist themes, and an admirer of the writers he treats in an article on the affair, deplores "the self-serving hyperbole, tendentiousness and Schadenfreude" of the opponents of de Man and deconstruction but concludes, "Still, the strained attempt to show that the early journalistic articles were occasions for admirable silence, powerful scenes of self-deconstruction or even acts of resistance itself unconsciously tends to lend credence to the charge that deconstruction can be used to justify or rewrite anything—a charge that most applies, in my judgment, to abuses of deconstruction from which no one is altogether immune."[103] In his critique of the apologetics of Jacques Derrida, Shoshana Felman, and Frederic Jameson,[104] LaCapra identifies their essential source, in psychoanalytic terms, as "transference," and he regrets their failure to "work through the trauma of distressing revelations by acknowledging and mourning the specific losses it involves." This approach patronizes their arguments, which in my view do not so much exemplify the presumption that deconstruction can be used "to justify or rewrite anything" as the assumption that any argument of a master rhetorician is self-validating.[105]

But to conjecture that the dubious arguments of these distinguished scholars reflect a failure of self-analysis, or the arrogance of the hermeneutically elect, or some other conscious or unconscious motives, is not to speak to the substance of their historical discourse. As this discourse claims the authority of conventional empirical and rational standards, there can be no reputable evasion of their requirements. Once committed to the rules of a certain game, one is responsible to those rules. I don't use the word "game" to trivialize the epistemological or ethical content of the argument. The people who are indignant over what they take to be misrepresentations of de Man's past are not simply choosing one set of rhetorical conventions over another; they are saying what they think is true and doing what they think is right. To observe this is not to deny the potential complexities in identifying facts relevant to a particular case, drawing appropriate inferences from them, or deriving plausible interpretations from the inferences. The complexities constitute the argument.

Chapter 4

Neither have I ever known a mind less sincere, nor one that had a more thorough contempt for the truth. When I say he [Alphonse de Lamartine] despised it, I am wrong: he did not honor it enough to heed it in any way whatever. When speaking or writing he spoke the truth or lied, without caring which he did, occupied only with the effect he wished to produce at the moment.

—Alexis de Tocqueville

Ronald Reagan's Bitburg Narrative

In the spring of 1985, the year of the fortieth anniversary of V-E Day, the defeat of the Nazis, and the liberation of the survivors of the death camps, President Ronald Reagan scheduled a trip to Germany at the invitation of Chancellor Helmut Kohl. On his visit to Washington the previous fall, the chancellor had invited the president to make a state visit to coincide with the economic summit scheduled in Bonn in May 1985. Among the sites suggested for the president's itinerary were the concentration camp at Dachau and the military cemetery at Bitburg. The president agreed to visit the cemetery but not the site of the camp.

When this schedule was announced, and when it was learned that a number of SS troops were buried at Bitburg, a wave of protest swept over the astonished White House. Not only groups predictably offended by such a gesture but also eighty-two senators, the American Legion, and various conservative groups urged the president to cancel the ceremony at the cemetery. Jewish organizations in the United States and abroad expressed shock, outrage, and pain. In an advertisement in the *New York Times*, 143 Christian leaders of various denominations, seminaries, and church councils also urged the president to cancel the ceremony. Reagan, who had originally defended his decision not to visit a concentration camp site by explaining that he did not wish to reopen the Germans' "great feelings of guilt," now decided to schedule a stop and a speech at Bergen-Belsen, the site of another camp.

This announcement did not still the protest, especially after the identification of forty-nine SS graves in the Bitburg cemetery. In perhaps the most dramatic expression of individual protest, Elie Wiesel, venerated voice of the survivors of the camps, took the occasion of a White House ceremony at which he was awarded the congressional Gold Medal of Achievement to implore the president to cancel the cemetery visit: "That place, Mr. President, is not your place. Your place is with the victims of the SS."

More responsive to the anguished plea of Chancellor Kohl not to renege on his commitment than to the arguments of his closest advisers, including his wife, Reagan held fast to the original itinerary. He conformed to the disputed schedule, delivered speeches at Bergen-Belsen and at the American Air Force base near Bitburg, and participated in a wreath-laying ceremony at the cemetery.

Ronald Reagan's defense of his pilgrimage to Bitburg in interviews and speeches amounted to a piecemeal narrative history of the German past and the Second World War that would provoke almost as much indignation as the trip itself.[1]

Reagan's justification for the Bitburg trip, told characteristically as a story, did not play well in the media. The *New York Times* declared, "America's oldest President displays America's shortest memory." According to *Time*, "Reagan displayed a curious insensitivity about the past, as if he did not know how important it is, or how dangerous it can be."[2]

What might be considered a preface to Reagan's historical apologia was presented in an interview in March 1985, when he explained why he did not intend to visit a concentration camp site during his German trip: "And I felt that, since the German people have very few alive that remember even the war, and certainly none of them who were adults and participating in any way, and, they do, they have a feeling, a guilt feeling that's been imposed upon them, and I just think it's unnecessary."[3] It is hard to find a category for this statement. It is so manifestly falsified by the very presence of the speaker, who was thirty years old in 1942 and who loved to recall his own stint in uniform, that it is difficult to identify some conscious intention to deceive. This was one occasion when saying what it felt good to say simply didn't come off.

Indeed, this version of the German population pyramid was soon revised to more or less plausible dimensions: "I grant you, there are some people there [in Germany] my age who remember the war and were participants in it on that side—but the bulk of the population, you might say everybody below 50 or 55, were either small children or not born yet."[4]

In light of this rectification, one might think of the first version as a momentary lapse into extremely careless historical demography, but the president's additional justification—that "I thought that the suggestion had come from an individual and was not a part of the state visit"—puts a considerable strain on credulity. According to George Shultz, then secretary of state, Dachau was "somewhat surprisingly" on the list of suggested sites handed over by Kohl at the time of the original invitation.[5]

At any rate, the intent that West Germany should not be plagued with painful reminders was clear enough. But considerably more than the predictable revision of this characteristic gaffe would be required: it quickly became apparent that there was no way that a visit to a German military cemetery could be anything but a reminder. The justification for the trip could not be confined to a celebration of the present and a happy forecast for the future; it would require an emollient reading of the past. This interpretation, pieced together from fragments in the president's speeches and interviews, constituted a historical narrative—a short story about the Nazi era.

The president's tale goes something like this: there was a time, now almost lost to living memory, when the German people came under the sway of an evil leader who unleashed the forces—"the awful evil started by one man"— that made the entire world (including the German people) his victim. The evil could only be ended with the destruction of that man through war. This war was fought against one man's totalitarian dictatorship but between gallant armies; the victors gave their lives to "rescue freedom in its darkest hour," and the defeated were as much victims of the despot who had drafted them into his armies—Reagan put the average age of the soldiers buried at Bitburg at eighteen—as any of those innocents (Anne Frank came to the president's mind) fed into his furnaces. The message to be drawn from the story of Anne Frank was one of hope: Reagan selected a passage from her diary in which she wrote, "I can feel the suffering of millions and yet, if I look up into the heavens I think that it will come right, that this cruelty will end and that peace and tranquility will return again." It is such a memory, Reagan says, that takes us "where God intended his children to go—toward learning, toward healing, and, above all, toward redemption." So the history of the war and the Holocaust is essentially a story with a happy ending. "The one lesson of World War II, the one lesson of Nazism, is that freedom must always be stronger than totalitarianism and that good must be stronger than evil." Out of overwhelming sorrow, God's purpose has been revealed, and (here Reagan draws on the Talmud) "out of ashes, hope." His hope and this redemption have been realized in the reconciliation of Germany and America: once implacable antagonists, now twin pillars of the free world.

The meaning of the president's story was also encapsulated in a fable—that is, a tale intended to exemplify a certain truth, to convey a moral. This is the story of German and American soldiers who strayed into a modest cottage "behind the lines" on Christmas Day. The old woman who lived there told them that shooting would not be tolerated in her home on that holy day, and she was obeyed. After partaking of a makeshift meal, "the battle-weary soldiers shook hands and went their separate ways."

This would all be rather confusing if one were possessed by the hobgoblin of petty accuracy, because the events were said to take place "as the Battle of the Bulge exploded not far away"—that is, in Belgium. Yet the cottage is apparently in Germany, as the woman risked the death penalty for sheltering the enemy and speaks some sort of German, "Komm, Herr Jesus, be our guest," she says. Whether Ronald Reagan or the *Reader's Digest* or some other source got it quite right, the message was clear enough. "Those boys reconciled briefly in the midst of war. Surely we allies in peacetime should honor the reconciliation of the last 40 years."

What is most objectionable about the story of the Christmas supper is not its implausibility but its interpretive implication. Historians often select an exemplary anecdote out of the welter of reconstructed events not only to focus the reader's imagination but also to advance an argument. The president's sentimental restaging of the poignant Christmas truce between the German and British lines in 1914 trivializes the horrendous moral dilemma of modern war—the coincidence of the simple instinct of human solidarity with the implacable dedication to mass destruction—to make the point that bygones should be bygones.

The president's historical pageant was concluded with a symbolic rendition of the "peace of the brave": two venerable paladins of the opposing forces, Generals Matthew Ridgeway and Johannes Steinhoff, shook hands by the German soldiers' graves in the Bitburg cemetery.

Many of those who objected to Ronald Reagan's narrative justification for his pilgrimage criticized it as bad history, as not only morally but epistemologically flawed. Can such an objection be sustained in the light of the sophisticated critique of historical discourse that conceives of narrative as a "cultural literary artifact at odds with the real"?[6] The problem, according to Louis Mink, is that "narrative form in history, as in fiction, is an artifice, the product of individual imagination. Yet at the same time it is accepted as claiming truth . . . as historical it [historical narrative] claims to represent, through its form, part of the real complexity of the past, but as narrative it is a product of imaginative construction, which cannot defend its claim to truth by any accepted procedure of argument or authentication." However, narrative does convey an interpretation, does make a point, does command an assent. As Richard McGuire puts it, "Authorial intention and logical criteria aside, if the audience is persuaded by a narration, it has *functioned* argumentatively for them."[7] The president's Bitburg tale was certainly intended to persuade.

Jerome Bruner, who characterizes narrative as "a version of reality whose acceptability is governed by convention and 'narrative necessity' rather than by empirical verification and logical requiredness," does note that "ironically we have no compunction about calling stories true or false."[8] This "irony," I believe, informs both our responses to stories told to us in daily intercourse and our responses to what our leaders tell us. And these judgments begin with our assessment of the factual validity of the narrative, to the extent that the narrator's claim to authority is epistemological.

Now it can be argued that this is scarcely where Reagan located his authority. Sidney Blumenthal remarked that the president was invulnerable to the incessant exposure of his factual errors in the national press because the journalist's empirical bedrock was not the plane from which the president operated. Reagan dealt in universals—in an ideology from which he inferred the "truth of facts." That is, the "facts" were means, and the ideology was served by any means necessary.[9] This interpretation might even be translated into postmodernese: empiricism is simply a language game that Reagan chose (quite successfully) not to play.

Still, each particular anecdote, argument, or narrative depended on the assumption that what was claimed to have happened actually did happen. For example, even if Reagan's tale of the humble cottage essentially functioned as a fable, if he had admitted, "That really didn't happen but I made it up to make my point," the anecdote's authority would have evaporated. Perhaps those who accepted Reagan's historical justification would have continued to accept it even if they couldn't quite swallow the Christmas fable; but the greater the number of assertions they perceived as false, the less their credence in the narrative's authority. Even if we believe that all historical narrative is part fiction,[10] we might conclude that this particular narrative contains too much fiction per history.

Yet, as Louis Mink argues, the assessment of the truth-value of narratives is not simply confined to the truth or falsity of the particular factual claims, "as a historical narrative claims truth not merely for each of its individual statements taken distributively, but for the complex form of the narrative itself."[11] This is where Hayden White's standards might apply. White might criticize Reagan's rhetoric as "inappropriate," as its mode of emplotment is comic. In White's lexicon, a comedy is a story that incarnates the "temporary triumph of man over his world"—that is, a story with a happy ending.[12] Many did object to Reagan's treatment of the Holocaust and the history of the Nazi era as a story with a happy ending. But the essential objections were to his misrepresentation of what had actually occurred, not only with reference to the facts of the case but also to the way he made historical sense of them.

Notably, the president's version of the Great (Bad) Man principle of historical explanation evoked responses ranging from indignation to contempt. A *Washington Post* editorial argued, "Nazi Germany was not, as Mr. Reagan seemed to suggest, the handiwork of 'one man' and his regime or even of hundreds or thousands. . . . It should come as no surprise that those who were prime victims of the Third Reich cannot support, let alone be enthusiastic about commemorations that necessarily so distort and degrade the terrible truths they know concerning the massive indifference and acquiescence that made their fate possible."[13] The editors were objecting not just to a morally offensive interpretation but to a historical perspective, recalcitrant to the immense accumulation of evidence on the active and passive implication of a large section of the German population in the program of extermination, and inadequate to our conception of how the world works. That is also why the assimilation of the German soldiers with the victims of the Holocaust is hermeneutically as well as epistemologically and morally flawed. Reagan's contribution to the history of the Nazi era makes it unintelligible.

The hostile response to the Bitburg story was itself the consequence of the history that Reagan attempted to depict, but reference to the historicity of the criticism does seem rather beside the point. To explore the parti pris of Elie Wiesel, or the *New York Times*, or the American Legion, or any of the critics of the president's narrative would scarcely mitigate its moral or epistemological flaws, just as reference to the obvious bias of the president's defenders, such as William Buckley, is no answer to their defense.

The commentary on the president's ad hoc defense of his itinerary is scarcely equivalent to the dense historical controversies treated in the preceding chapters, but it does provide a somewhat different perspective on the issues considered there. On what grounds do we grant authority to any representation of any past, and therefore on what grounds do we refuse authority? Can the authority be located in the effectiveness of the representation—that is, on how it worked for the audience it was intended to persuade? If its effectiveness depends on its claim to truthful reconstruction, can its success exempt it from an objective assessment of the claim?

Effectiveness was certainly a key criterion for Reagan's public discourse, characteristically conveyed in anecdotes, reminiscences, and exemplary tales. The remarkable success of that pragmatic historical rhetoric has been celebrated by his admirers, including those who deplore the decline of classical standards of objectivity in the classroom, and denounced by his critics, including those who doubt the authority of conventional criteria of historical veridicality.

In his introduction to *Bitburg in Moral and Political Perspective*, a collection of responses to and reflections on the issue, Geoffrey Hartman observed, "'Bitburg' disclosed that what understanding there was at the highest level of government led not to sensitivity, but only to sentimentality. For even if Mr. Reagan was being shielded from too close a contact with the emotional side of things, straight historical truths were not getting through, and this meant an astonishing ignorance or lack of interest on the part of his advisors."[14] Hartman, member of the Department of Comparative Literature and director of the Video Archive for Holocaust Testimonies at Yale, has long been associated with literary and philosophic movements that "destabilize" any simple confidence in "straight historical truths." There might seem to be a considerable distance between, for example, Hartman's abstruse reflections on "the impossibility of making truth and text coincide"[15] and the travesty of historical truth in Reagan's Bitburg text, but to question the possibility of the truthfulness of texts in general does undermine the grounds for refuting particular political lies.

This point has been put in stronger terms by Russell Berman:

Deconstruction has participated in the conservative hegemony in a further and more crucial manner, close to the heart of the Reaganite legacy. For Reaganism was not at all, primarily, a matter of a triumphant cultural conservatism of the sort advocated by Bennett or Helms, no matter how much such figures mobilized and exploited archaic sentiments in parts of the electorate. The hallmark of Reaganism lay elsewhere: the definitive entrenchment of a manipulative media politics, the displacement by image of content or substance, an extensive aestheticization of politics and everyday life. Rhetoric and style, rather than coherence or even reference, have become the important parameters of political theater. No wonder that a theory of language that preaches the dogma of non-referentiality could attain plausibility in that setting of universal mendacity. The deconstructive rejection of any communicative capacity in language is the philosophical justification of the presidential *parole*. The celebration of rhetoric is the heart and soul of the culture of speechwriters. The doctrine of the free-floating signifier is the transubstantiation of the Teflon presidency: beyond good and evil, beyond logocentrism, and beyond congressional subpoena.[16]

Berman could be read as transforming chronological coincidence into a cultural conspiracy, but I prefer to read him as underlining the parallel implications of a certain theoretical destabilizing of the truth and a certain practical disregard for it.

To approach this issue from another angle: for those who believe that "a rational stance is itself a stance of oppression or domination, and accepted ideals of reason both reflect and reinforce power relations that advantage white privileged men,"[17] what better place to register the absence of white, male, middle-class standards of rationality and objectivity than the Reagan White House—complete with astrology?[18] Well, that *is* a bit too categorical. If rationality is defined as an appropriate matching of means to ends, such as redistributing income upward or shifting resources from welfare to weaponry, in his first term at least, Reagan seemed to have discovered the philosopher's stone. The regime's rhetoric too might be considered rational if "rationality" denotes "persuasion by any means necessary." But if we conceive of rationality as adherence to certain familiar standards of factual accuracy and logical coherence, and objectivity as an adherence to those standards irrespective of other preferences, they were scarcely the preferred instruments of gender, racial, or class dominance during the twelve years of Republican administration.[19]

I believe that in his presidential role, Ronald Reagan was probably less honest than his predecessors or successors, but I grant that he had ample precedent. Lying to the public was not invented in 1981. Raised though I was in the faith of Franklin Delano Roosevelt, I must acknowledge that great man's genial duplicity. And since the Second World War, official discourse, especially in the realm of foreign affairs, has been characterized by the confusion of secrecy that serves national security with the manipulation of facts to suit the public relations needs of the current administration. When Ronald Reagan assumed office, plausible deniability lay to hand. For almost forty years, the Cold War had provided a blanket justification for lying for the health of the state.

Thus Sidney Hook could defend the CIA's surreptitious funding of the Congress for Cultural Freedom and *Encounter* magazine: "Yes, there was an element of deception in not making public what we knew or suspected. In war even more deplorable deceptions are accepted even by the most honorable. Even in peacetime no one feels impelled to tell the whole truth about everything."[20] Not the standard he would have applied during the Moscow Purge Trials.

In a book titled *The Politics of Lying*, published in 1973, David Wise remarked on the loss of public trust in the presidency, perceived as a "system of institutionalized lying" in the name of national security. Wise recalls that point in the Kennedy administration when "an Assistant Secretary of Defense proclaimed the right to lie."[21] That official was Arthur Sylvester, who subsequently defended his widely criticized statement with references to "circumstances that impelled responsible leaders to assume the burden of falsehood to protect their countrymen," or to "deceive a potential enemy."[22]

By the time Sylvester's justification for lying for the common weal appeared in the *Saturday Evening Post*, the United States was at war in Vietnam, and those in high office found it necessary to deceive their fellow citizens about policies that were well-known to the enemy. In fact, as early as 1954 our government was sending psy-war and paramilitary teams into North Vietnam (in violation of our pledge to refrain from threat or use of force), where most of them were liquidated by the "enemy." As Senator Mike Gravel would subsequently observe in his introduction to the *Pentagon Papers*, "The enemy knew what we were not permitted to know."[23]

Thus there were many precedents for such "covert" Reagan administration operations as the mining of the harbors of Nicaragua and other deceptions of the American public, Congress, and appropriate congressional committees. And in domestic policy, too, examples of what is now called "disinformation" lie thick on the political ground of those years before 1981.[24] What sets Reagan apart is the phenomenal success of his instrumental approach to matters of fact. The invulnerability of that particular atruthful mix of genuine sincerity, apparent sincerity, and chronic mendacity has sustained a rich literature of fascinated and puzzled commentary.

In 1983 Mark Green and Gail MacColl published a compendium of quotations to illustrate their assertion that "no modern President has engaged in so consistent a pattern of misspeaking on such a wide range of subjects—and shown no sense of remorse." These were errors "far more serious than *faux pas*—obvious exaggerations, material omissions, contrived anecdotes, voodoo statistics, denial of unpleasant facts, and flat untruths."[25] This collection found a sufficient market for Green and MacColl to tap the rich presidential vein in a sequel in 1987.[26] If you ask for these volumes in a bookstore (to no effect, in my experience—the publishers, Pantheon Books, say they are out of stock), you will be directed to the section labeled "Humor." And that is how the works present themselves—small (7″-by-7″) volumes printed on shiny paper, with risible pictures of Reagan on the cover and, in the text, subtitles such as "Wishful Thinking Department," "Little Known Fun Fact," "Tall Tale." The contents, however, are meticulously documented examples drawn from a vast pool of exaggerations, distortions, and flat untruths, and are presented with genuine indignation.

The discrepancy between the format of these books—comic—and the content—tragic, or at least profoundly depressing for any partisan of democratic leadership—is one version of the ambivalent response to the performance of that immensely popular, politically unbeatable Teflon president. In what has become a vast literature of analysis and reconstruction of the Reagan era, the characterization of Reagan as the embodiment of atruthfulness, somewhat on the lines of Tocqueville's portrayal of Lamartine, has become a commonplace even among his supporters, if not always in the sardonic language of a hostile outsider like Alexander Cockburn: "Reagan, the actor, has absolutely no moral sense about truth or falsity. Truth, to him, is what he happens to be saying at the time. Even when he is repeating some hoary old lie about welfare cheats which has been exposed in the press a hundred times, he still looks as though he is telling truth. I'm sure he thinks he is telling the truth."[27]

It has become standard practice to cite those many examples of sincere misrepresentation—those anecdotes such as the heroic commander who goes down with his bomber, winning an imaginary congressional Medal of Honor (traced to the 1944 Dana Andrews movie *A Wing and a Prayer*);[28] arguments fortified by anecdotes from events in his own past that never occurred; the opportunistic citation of imaginary statistics—all apparently with genuine conviction. Some of Reagan's recollections, however, put a strain on the theory of unwitting misrepresentation. In November 1983 he told a delegation of Israelis that he had seen the devastation of the Holocaust himself while filming the liberation of the concentration camps, whereas in reality, all of the filming that he did during that period was in the Army Air Corps picture unit in Hollywood. This episode required considerable spin control by his retinue. If that was a sincere mistake, one begins to suspect delusion rather than carelessness.[29]

And then there were plenty of "flat untruths"—statements known by the speaker to be false.[30] These uncharacteristically shocked and offended the public during the Iran-contra affair, when Reagan lied on a scale that was close to a parody of falsification as *raison d'état*. The last of this series of categorical falsehoods—that there was no third nation involved in the arms transfer—was officially repudiated twenty minutes after Reagan had presented it.[31]

My point is not to redocument what has become a virtual commonplace description of Reagan in operation, or to contribute one more interpretation of what he was really all about, or to try to unmask the real Ronald Reagan. It is to re-pose this question: in the light of skepticism about stable standards for judging historical truth or valid representations of the past, how are we to think about political lies? What are the standards according to which one might refute Ronald Reagan's dubious narratives? If "no facts demonstrably correspond to a historical reality," if "traditional criteria of truth and falsity do not apply to representations of the past," on what scale do we weigh the facts fabricated for the political needs of the president?[32]

President Reagan can be distinguished from his predecessors by the extent to which this question seemed to require a defensive gloss from his servants and supporters. In most of the volumes written by former satraps at the Reagan White House in the attempt to understand their enigmatic chief, there is usually some portion devoted to an explication of what are often referred to as his "gaffes" or "inaccuracies." At one end of a spectrum that ranges from effusion to disillusion, we have Edwin Meese's assertion that Reagan generally got it right: "In fact, he [Ronald Reagan] had a remarkably retentive memory, recalling things that he had read years before to make a current point. (This greatly annoyed his detractors who, unaware of the matters he would cite, would automatically—and erroneously—assume they were incorrect.)"[33] A more common view, also held by some of Reagan's critics, was that although he was wrong from time to time, he was always sincere. Lyn Nofziger recalled, "Unlike most politicians, whenever he took a stand on an issue, he believed his was right. Even though he might flip-flop on it, he did so on belief not expediency."[34]

Donald Regan portrayed the president as a man who absorbed a remarkable amount of information and stored it in a powerful but uncritical memory system. This memory system was what led to "his gaffes and misstatements in encounters with the press. . . . It never seemed to occur to him that anyone would give him incorrect information. His mind was a trove of facts and anecdotes, something like the morgue of one of his favorite magazines, *Reader's Digest,* and it was impossible to guess when or why he might access any one of these million bytes of data."[35]

Reflecting on the president's denial that arms had been traded to Iran for hostages, George Shultz concluded,

> The president's speech convinced me that Ronald Reagan still truly did not believe that what had happened had, in fact, happened. To him the reality was different. I had seen him like this before on other issues. He would go over the "script" of an event, past or present, in his mind, and once that script was mastered, that was the truth—no fact, no argument, no plea for reconsideration, could change his mind. So what Reagan said to the American people was true to him, although it was not the reality.[36]

Michael Deaver, the impresario of marketing the presidential image in the first term, thought that if Reagan had a problem with the press, it was his inability to deceive. "He may be flat wrong, he may embellish an anecdote, but he finds it inconceivable that anyone would accuse him of lying." This insight is followed by an anecdote describing something remarkably like a "flat untruth." During the New Hampshire campaign, candidate Reagan told an ethnic joke guaranteed to offend Poles and Italians. When the press taxed him for this, he said that he had told the joke as an example of the offensiveness of ethnic jokes and promised to tell only Irish jokes in the future. To answer those critics who seemed to believe that "for Reagan reality and myths often blur" and that Reagan often borrowed stories about his own wartime experience from films, Deaver drew a fine distinction: "Reagan is a romantic, not an impostor. When he talks about seeing the bodies of Holocaust victims piled like firewood, he may or may not have explained he had been viewing the footage shipped home by the Signal Corps. (He saw this nightmare on film, not in person. That did not mean he saw it less.)"[37]

In *What I Saw at the Revolution*, Peggy Noonan, a clever speechwriter for Reagan and Bush, takes up the theme of reality and myth to identify the president as a paragon of contemporary culture. In a section entitled "We Are All Actors Now," Noonan characterized our entire society as on stage; from Ollie North to Gary Hart to the man at the Amoco station or the woman at the little store, everyone is cast into a role, and the Reagans are best of all: "They are at their best when they are performing. Increasingly this is true of their countrymen." But Reagan's rhetoric went beyond playacting to strike an even more profound chord in the American psyche: it transcended fact to attain the character of myth.

> They said he lived by symbols and mythic figures and that's why he was so drawn to those *Reader's Digest* stories about the airman who went down with the wounded gunner, and why he was so moved by movies.
>
> But in turning to myth wasn't he being American? Johnny Appleseed, Paul Bunyan, Casey Jones—a hundred years ago when we were settling the West and families full of children close in age were living by themselves, with no one else for miles, no one else within sight—a huge lonely country telling itself stories in isolated cabins, a huge lonely country going to the movies and believing what it saw, that Ty Power was brave and Spence strong, a huge lonely country turning on TV and shooting the existential breeze with Ralph Kramden and Rowdy Yates and then . . . Reagan.
>
> Who understood the loneliness, knew it in his bones, and wanted to assuage it. For eight years he did.[38]

In breathtaking juxtaposition to this celebration of storytelling, consider Noonan's reflections on Bush's defeat in the November 5, 1992, issue of the *New York Times*: "The worst thing is to lie to the people, but the second worst is to ignore them and not tell them what you are doing and why."

Analysis of Reagan's relation to historical truth has not been confined to the critics who excoriate it or the admirers who find euphemisms for it. Lou Cannon, a columnist for the *Washington Post*, who devoted his journalistic career to covering Ronald Reagan critically but sympathetically, drew on the insights of the psychologist Howard Gardner—a theorist of "multiple intelligences"—to characterize Reagan's intelligence as one that "makes sense of the world narratively." Cannon regarded this system as the avenue to understanding that Reagan was "intelligent but on his own terms."[39]

Others have also characterized Reagan as making sense of the world, and of the past, through narrative, through telling stories. According to William F.

Lewis, "Stories are not just a rhetorical device that Reagan uses to embellish his ideas; Reagan's message is a story. Reagan uses story-telling to direct his policies, ground his explanation, and inspire his audiences, and the dominance of narrative helps to account for the variety of reactions to his rhetoric." The force of the president's narrative depended not on the validity of its factual constituents but on its coherence in expressing, or urging changes in, a simple but powerful myth: "America is a chosen nation, grounded in its families and neighborhoods, and driven inevitably forward by its heroic working people toward a world of freedom and economic progress unless blocked by moral or military weakness." Inaccuracies or falsehoods that illustrate the myth—that serve the particular story—do not lessen its effect, which depends on "a narrative logic that emphasizes the connection between character and action, not a rational logic that emphasizes the connections between problems and solutions." Charges of ignorance or factual error never affected Reagan's popularity or credibility, because "the basis for accepting the referential value of Reagan's stories is not empirical justification, but consistency with the moral standards and common sense of his audience." Therefore the only effective challenge, at least at the peak of Reagan's popularity, might have been a counter-myth, such as that expressed by Mario Cuomo.[40]

Thus Peggy Noonan's chic and cynical insertion of Ronald Reagan into the great American tradition of folk mythology strikes a familiar chord. Myth, as a vital constituent of social coherence, or moral transformation, has long been justified from what might be called a Sorelian-pragmatic perspective. According to this system, the question is not "were the president's public statements true," but "how did they work?" From this perspective, when Ronald Reagan said "America is back"—put it across with his phenomenal delivery—he was believed, and America *was* back, with a general recovery of national pride and collective self-respect. According to some analysts of political leadership, "one of the major achievements of the Reagan administration must be the contribution it made to the renewal of trust in American national government. The President's charisma—combining as it did Reagan's relaxed style, good humor, decisiveness and faith in the eternal verities, with an ability to communicate a strong sense of pride in the nation—was the dominant factor in the process."[41]

In this scholarly assessment of the "Reagan legacy," trust is severed from truthfulness. Where the hallmark is plausibility rather than integrity, the pragmatic standard, as in, for example, the polemic of the anti-Dreyfusards—does not distinguish the effects of lies from the consequences of lying. The phenomenally effective blend of style and more or less spurious substance, the mastery of the mass media that immunized Reagan against criticism of his misrepresentations, contributed to the "success" granted by many critics as well as supporters of his policies.[42] However, an assessment of the consequences for American political culture cannot be confined to an estimate of the political payoff in the short term. Robert Hughes strikes a different balance: "With somnambulistic efficiency, Reagan educated American down to his level. He left his country a little stupider in 1988 than it had been in 1980, and a lot more tolerant of lies, because his style of image-presentation cut the connective tissue between ideas and hence fostered the defeat of thought itself."[43]

The celebration of political pragmatism often assumes what remains to be demonstrated. What "works" or is "good in the way of belief" from one perspective is someone else's Vulgar Pragmatism serving the wrong good. For some commentators, Reagan's narrative defense of his Bitburg trip did him no lasting harm, so there was little left to criticize. For others the harm was in the narrative itself.

One approach transcends the issue of politico-historical falsification by hermeneuticizing it—political analysis writ French. In one of her more intelligible passages, Diane Rubenstein tells us that "Reagan as a synecdoche, is a microcosmic replication of American culture," or "a stand-in for the rest of American culture." The challenge of Reagan's presidency to historical representation "is addressed by European theorists of hyper-realism and simulation who see America as the home of absolute fake and artificial restoration."[44] This is the America of Umberto Eco, where "the 'completely real' becomes identified with the 'completely fake'"; or of Jean Baudrillard, where "cinema is true because it is the whole of space, the whole way of life that are cinematic. The break between the two, the abstraction which we deplore, does not exist: life is cinema." And, Baudrillard asks, "all societies end up wearing masks. Why not the mask of Reagan?"[45]

Setting aside the magisterial reductionisms, there is something to all of this. The American public would not have responded to Reagan's music if there were no chords to be struck. Commentators in all camps have registered his remarkable ability to liberate his audience—or a significant section of his audience—from reality, in just the way it wanted to be liberated.[46] The public that during the Iran hostage crisis of 1980 carried placards simply lettered JOHN WAYNE, or made a hero of Oliver North not despite of but *because* of his lies, shared an ethic for which truth runs a poor second to consequences and in which consequences are identical to wishes.

The president found a receptive public for the sort of falsification that is not even intended to deceive. Various disclaimers of widely reported interventions in Nicaragua simply provided a minuscule fig leaf for Congress. This sort of cognitive dissonance is familiar enough in a sports-loving society that embraces the NCAA's dedication to the academic progress of major-league athletes, who are forced to undergo higher education if they wish to enter professional sports through the farm clubs in the colleges and universities.

Diane Rubenstein concludes that in a culture characterized by an acceptance of the signs of the real for the real itself and by the blurring of facts and fiction, Ronald Reagan's bizarre rendering of history "cannot be judged on the basis of truth or accuracy."[47] However, "hyper-reality" does not completely characterize American political culture—that is, you can't fool all of the people all of the time. The magic failed for a considerable proportion of Reagan's audience during his Iran-contra fabrications and the historical narrative he composed to justify his ceremonial journey to the German military cemetery.

These stories threw even some of Reagan's staunchest supporters into a state of ambivalence. George Shultz, who thought the original decision to go to Bitburg was a disastrous mistake but praised the president for sticking to his guns, couldn't quite resist quoting objections to a moral balance sheet that equated "victims with perpetrators," or citing the fact that many of those buried at Bitburg, including veteran members of the SS, had been born before 1920.[48]

For Midge Decter, a major contributor to *Commentary*, the combative voice of the conservative intelligentsia published by the American Jewish Committee, the president's march into a "moral minefield" was an especially distressing detour.[49] Not that Decter's distress over Reagan's blunder in 1985 undermined her loyalty to the successful executor of the conservative agenda. In her review of Reagan's last autobiography, published eight years after Bitburg, she celebrated the author as someone who had been able to "say simple things" when they needed saying.[50] It is not likely that the president's justification for his Bitburg visit was one of those simple things. In her August 1985 essay, Decter did manage a dialectical tour de force that had Reagan proceeding from the premises of his liberal antagonists, but the burden of her piece was a severe and eloquent indictment of his historical distortions and irresponsible fabrications.

On selected occasions, such as Bitburg or the Iran-contra affair, the ambivalence of the Reaganite intelligentsia amounted to something like a self-performed lobotomy, not simply because they happened to disagree with a given policy but because they too were asked to swallow whatever mixture of plausible anecdote, half-truth, and blatant falsehood was concocted for the occasion. The flexible standards required of Reagan loyalists are still embraced by the conservative Cassandras of the decline of higher education in America, for whom skepticism as to objective truth in the university is a threat to civilization as we have known it, and mendacity in the office of the (right) president is a bagatelle. Robert Hughes puts it this way: "The loss of reality by euphemism and lies was twenty times worse and more influential in the utterances of the last two Presidents and their aides than among *bien-pensant* academics, although you didn't find any complaints about that in *Commentary* or the *New Criterion*."[51]

One would scarcely expect complaints from the regime's cultural proconsuls, including, for a notorious example, William Bennett. Or from Dinesh D'Souza, whose campaign for rational and humane discourse on the American campus[52] was launched from his editorial chair at the *Dartmouth Review*. Nor would we expect the conservative historian Gertrude Himmelfarb, a Reagan appointee to the council of the National Endowment for the Humanities (NEH), whose recent book is "dedicated to the proposition that there are such things as truth and reality and that there is a connection between them,"[53] to have emphasized the disjunction between reality and Reagan's brand of truth.

Or take Martin Anderson, a member of the brain trust in Reagan's first administration, now a fellow at the Hoover Institution and a contributor to the growth industry of exposés of the intellectual and moral corruption of the American professorate in general and left deconstructionists in particular. As an example of their "grotesque reasoning," Anderson cites Paul de Man's alleged repudiation of any preference between truth and error.[54] This is not a distinction Anderson was at pains to draw when he was serving Reagan, or celebrating him in his memoir of the Reagan-era "revolution." In that book there is not the least mention of the president's odd relation to the truth. Even in assigning him some responsibility for the arms-to-Iran fiasco (things seem to have gone downhill after Anderson left the administration), Anderson makes no reference whatsoever to the series of falsifications with which Reagan met the crisis.[55]

Republican appointees to the chair of the NEH felt a special obligation to defend national culture from the excesses of political correctness and ultra-relativism. In his summary of the 1984 report of the Study Group on the State of Learning in the Humanities in Higher Education, William Bennett identified, among other alarming tendencies in academe, the fact that there was "no longer agreement on the value of historical facts, empirical evidence, or even rationality itself."[56] This theme is pursued in his book *The De-Valuing of America*, which exposes that large group of "today's intellectuals" who "have overstepped the bounds of common sense and seem to have given up on the disinterested pursuit of truth. They have hitched their intellect to the service of ideology." Such were the intellectuals, predominant in the liberal university elite, who massively repudiated President Reagan, a man of immovable solidity who articulated the common sense of the American people through the concrete representation of "a story, an anecdote, a recollection of things past."

No reference here as to whether the president got the recollection right. During the Iran-contra crisis, when Reagan's recollections were not so much quasi-fictional reminiscences as common garden-variety lies, Bennett is proud to have rallied to his leader's standard when many supporters "headed for the tall grass." In the darkest days, Bennett urged the president not to allow himself to accept humiliation but to explain "what he had done and why" and "assume responsibility for his own acts." The president agreed that he would do just that, "accept this responsibility, and move on to other things."[57] And so he did. The president said, "A few months ago I told the American people I did not trade arms for hostages. My heart and my best intentions tell me that is true, but the facts and the evidence tell me it is not."[58]

Bennett's successor at the NEH, Lynne Cheney, carried on the crusade. In the final report of her tenure, entitled *Telling the Truth*, Cheney quotes, as a horrible example of the willful abandonment of the pursuit of truth, a manifesto by Somekawa and Smith that argues, "Historians should assess an argument on the basis of its persuasiveness, its potential utility, and its political sincerity"—precisely the grounds for which Ronald Reagan's political rhetoric has been celebrated by those whose ends he served.[59] There is an irony in this reference that cuts both ways: for Somekawa and Smith, because it seems unlikely that any criticism of Reagan's politics or his mendacity would be disarmed for them by a recognition that he had successfully applied their precepts; for Cheney, because he actually subverted what she ostensibly defended.

During her tenure at the endowment, Lynne Cheney was hailed by George Will as "the secretary of domestic defense, fighting more sinister adversaries than those that her husband Dick had to face in defense of our national intellectual legacy."[60] Will, who himself had done valiant battle against the cultural Visigoths, concluded his retrospective assessment of the Reagan regime with a eulogy of its leader—the "captain who calmed the sea"—and of the rhetoric that had been central to Reagan's presidency:

> His aim had been to restore the plain language of right and wrong, good and evil, for the purpose of enabling people to make the most of freedom. In his long career of crisscrossing the country, practicing the exacting ethic of democratic persuasion, he has resembled a political John Wesley. For all his deplorable inattentiveness regarding many aspects of his office, he has been assiduous about nurturing a finer civic culture, as he understands it. Here, then, is the crowning paradox of Reagan's career. For all his disparagement of government, he has given it the highest possible purpose, the improvement of the soul of the nation.[61]

Apparently, the "ethic of democratic persuasion" has no particular relation to truth, and a finer civic culture is best nurtured through manipulation of the mass media.

I am one of the "innumerable academics" characterized in Alan Ryan's review of Robert Hughes's *The Culture of Complaint*: "There are innumerable academics who believe, as Hughes does, that any Republican who complains of the academic radicals' contempt for the concept of truth must have been fast asleep while Reagan and Bush were lying their heads off; and who believe, at the same time, that intellectuals who give up on the very idea of truth are committing *trahison des clercs* of the worst kind."[62] A certain conservative intelligentsia and what might be called the postmodernist academic Left coincide in the radical disjunction of how truth is to be considered in, and out of, the academy. For university-based politically conscious scholars, the indeterminacy of all discourse does not absolve liars in the political arena; for the intellectual Right, the sinister subversion of truth in the university has nothing to do with mendacity in the real world, at least when the right people are telling the lies.

Conclusion

The temptation is to fall into the trap of concluding that all rational argument

is mere rationalization and then proceeding to try to argue rationally for this

position.—Hilary Putnam

A familiar criticism of philosophizing about historical literature, especially when the philosophy is imbued with a positivist taint, is that it ignores what historians actually do—how they conduct research and write their histories. My intention has been to examine how people concerned with certain controversial pasts have actually told their stories and validated their claims. "People," because the controversies were not confined to professional historians, and because I believe that the same issues regarding valid histories are involved when anyone reconstructs, interprets, or argues about any past up to and including yesterday.

It would not require a subtle textual analysis to expose the disembodied authorial voice through which I "privilege" explicit and unstated assumptions about objective truth and moral right. I affirm that Stalinist narratives were conscious falsifications; that certain Dreyfusards were admirable in their commitment to the truth, according to my criteria of truth; that an apologetic "setting the record straight" on the wartime writings of Paul de Man depended on self-serving and self-contradictory statements; that a mendacious presidency is politically unhealthy and morally deplorable; and that I can specify the mendacity under certain circumstances.

I acknowledge that my standards are not independent of my personal identity, my loyalties, and the language in which I think. But I believe that such observations, while "true," are vacuous until the critic indicates wherein he or she disagrees with my criteria of veridicality. If the disagreements are so fundamental that the criteria are incommensurable, then the conversation stops. But the conversation never does stop. I don't want to go into the question as to whether any communication between humans is ultimately incommensurable, as the parties to the conversations considered in this book all appealed to common criteria for the truth-content of historical propositions, especially when claiming to refute lies about the past.

The common claims to cognitive authority speak to the vexed issue of historical objectivity, because the parties to those politically charged historical controversies assumed that an intellectually reputable member of the community they wished to persuade would necessarily accede to rational and empirically grounded argument irrespective of other preferences; or, to put it another way, that there was a moral obligation to be objective.

The reference to the common claims is not intended to affirm some universal ground of historical truth—some "God's eye point of view" of history (to borrow from Hilary Putnam[1])—but to identify the conceptual schemes according to which historical authority was claimed. One might argue, then, from the perspective of philosophers such as Richard Rorty or Donald Davidson, that the preceding cases simply provide examples of the "widespread sharing of sentences held true by speakers of the same language."[2]

This is true to the extent that all parties to the controversies—even Barrès—did claim the authority of relevant evidence, plausible inference, and logical coherence. My concern, however, is not to cite this practical consensus as if to lay the foundations for an ideal speech community or to rest my case on a sort of epistemological deism, identifying some irreducible minimum of universally accepted, if undemonstrable, criteria of historical veracity, but to expose the tension between conventional rational and empirical criteria and other tacit or explicit claims to historical authority, especially as these exhibited the polemical bad faith of the simultaneous appeal to conflicting claims.

The most obvious, and dubious, claim rests on the appeal to *an* authority—a presumably infallible person, group, community, or institution. This is often a tacit appeal, because the warrant of the authority cannot stand alone, especially when the antagonists do not grant the premise. In the political universe where to contradict Stalin was *lèse majesté*, it was still necessary to demonstrate wherein he was always right. The anti-Dreyfusard conviction of the competence and integrity of the officer corps eventually had to be buttressed by the authority of Bertillon's "demonstrations" that Dreyfus had cleverly forged his own handwriting. To put Paul de Man's wartime collaborationism into proper postmodern perspective, the authority of a coterie of "attentive readers" was fortified by arguments designed to set the historical record straight. The immense personal authority of Ronald Reagan, implicit in the delivery of whatever "truth" served the immediate purpose, could not dispense with the assumption that what he happened to be saying was, in fact, the case.

The claim to an inherent personal or collective authority is often accompanied by the explicit identification of the opponent's bias. Recent theorizing about historical discourse dignifies this approach as the recognition of the "historicity" of everyone's presumption of historical or any other sort of veridicality. As Joan Scott sees it, one cannot justify "history aimed at producing subjects without interrogating and relativizing the means of their production."[3] When historical issues are sharpened to a political point, "interrogating and relativizing" usually comes down to arguments ad hominem and the identification of the corrupt motives that lie behind the rationalizations of someone else's interest. Various versions of the good old Marxist "It is no accident that" avoid the need to refute an argument by identifying its antecedents.[4]

Stalinists and fellow travelers tried to preempt the judgment of the Dewey Commission by exposing its Trotskyite bias. As their factual case collapsed, it became increasingly necessary for the anti-Dreyfusards to invent and reinvent the implacable animus of a conspiracy that undermined their cause. Reference to the self-interest of the opposing camp was a recurrent theme in the debate over the wartime writings of Paul de Man. The appeal to motive was reversed in the commentary on Ronald Reagan, whose admirers appealed to his virtuous motives to justify his mélange of fantasy and falsification.

When truth claims about the past are undermined with reference to someone's specific bias, or in the light of a general skepticism about anyone's objectivity, or with reference to the "historicity" of any standard of veridicality, it is invariably presumed that the critic is exempt from the same charge. This is the case even when the critique includes a disclaimer that relativizes the critic's own standards, because at some point the critic cashes the warrant for assent to his or her claim. Whether in crude argument ad hominem or in the subtle application of a selective pyrrhonism or a self-exempting sociology of knowledge, the essential point of the critique is the polemical payoff.

The criterion of the payoff is also implicated in the identification of historical truths in the light of their consequences. The strongest version of this definition of truth, argued, for example, by the anti-Dreyfusards, is not simply to prefer truths with desirable consequences but to believe that the consequences constitute the truth. Hayden White seems to say this when he argues that the truth of a given claim—in this instance the Zionist interpretation of the Holocaust—"consists precisely in its effectiveness."[5] This line has been sharply criticized by Carlo Ginzburg, among others, because it potentially reduces the criterion of truth to the argument of the strongest party and because it logically subsumes what is ordinarily called a lie.[6]

For me, the indeterminate relationship between effectiveness and truth highlights my difficulty in understanding quite what is meant by the pragmatic standard for historical truth. Perhaps the conviction I share with Appleby, Hunt, and Jacob—that "no list of good consequences can redeem the false-ness of a proposition"[7]—is a moral choice that preempts the grounds for debate with someone who believes that good consequences constitute the truth of a proposition, or that any such standard justifies what are ordinarily called lies. Apparently this isn't what contemporary pragmatists have in mind; indeed, Appleby and her coauthors also affirm pragmatism as "vital to the kind of history we are advocating."[8] Their brand of pragmatism does not attempt to identify the truth in the results but rather recognizes that all truths can be provisional in theory while rejecting the relativism inherent in question-ing all claims in principle. It is certainly easy to agree with that, or with Michael Roth's observation, "A sense of tolerance, as American pragmatists have been arguing for more than one hundred years now, does not make it impossible to stand up for what you believe."[9] But aside from the evident virtue in refusing to send for the thought police, in what sense does such a pragmatism answer John Dewey's question regarding "the grounds on which some judgments about a course of past events are more entitled to credence than certain other ones"? In the cases considered in this book, if the pragmatic standard does not refer to specific political consequences of a certain reading of the past, to what does it refer? In any case, the pragmatic standards simply relocate the question: on what grounds? By whose authority?

Appleby, Hunt, and Jacob locate this authority in a group—an academic dis-cipline, perhaps, or, more broadly, all the members of a political democracy—although they fear that this criterion exposes the critical intellectual to the tyranny of the majority.[10] However, the decision to tell the truth according to one's own lights is not to be exposed to tyranny but to freely associate with those who speak the same language. When the political chips are down, stories about the past will continue to command our assent when they proceed from shared assumptions as to relevant evidence, legitimate inference, and coherent logic. We cannot validate these standards by appealing to them, but there is no need to validate them if the parties to the conversations share them. Of course people of goodwill, sharing the same standards, will continue to differ about the past, which is to say that history is not mathematics—and even mathematics is fuzzy around the edges.

Appendix A

Letter from Paul de Man to Harvard Authorities

Harvard University   Boston, January 26th 1955
Cambridge, Massachusetts   30 McLean Street

Dear Professor Poggioli:

I understand that, following my application for a passport to go abroad, the Society of Fellows has received information of a highly derogatory nature regarding my past history. I gladly take the opportunity which is given me to clarify and to explain my situation. The matters that have arisen seem to fall under the following headings:

(1) modalities of my admission at Harvard and of my election to the Society

(2) conditions under which I entered this country and my present status with the Department of Immigration

(3) my political past, particularly under the German occupation

(4) legal charges brought against me as a result of the liquidation of a publishing-firm to which I was attached.

I will deal with these matters in this order.

(1) I was admitted to the graduate school of Arts and Sciences Department of Comparative Literature by Professor Poggioli in September 1952. During the previous year, I had had informal contacts with Professor Levin and during the Spring I decided, on my own initiative, to apply for admission. My admission was based on the following data:

(a) an undergraduate degree in Chemical Science from the University of Brussels from 1940

(b) references from colleagues at Bard College, where I taught for two years previously to coming to Boston, in particular from Mr. Ted Weiss and Joseph Summers, now at the University of Connecticut

(c) a literary paper which I had given to Prof. Levin and which he had passed on to Prof. Poggioli, a first draft, in fact, of the very project on which I am working now.

In my application, I pointed out that there had been a change in my academic career from science to the humanities, and I stated my continuous interest in literary problems, as it appeared from writing I had done, from the courses I taught at Bard, etc. I never invoked any other titles or documents; I did not claim any graduate credits and did not apply for the scholarship that I sorely needed, estimating that, since nobody at Harvard knew me well, I first had to prove myself. The financial strain of having to pay tuition and support my family without any outside help was extremely hard. Throughout my two years as a graduate student, I earned a living by teaching languages at the Berlitz School, by translations, readings for a publisher, etc. In my second year, a teaching fellowship eased the financial burden somewhat, though not that of overwork.

Professor Poggioli admitted me "on trial," precisely because there had been a shift in my field of study and also because my application came in quite late. That term, I could only afford to take two courses and the Graduate School does not allow students admitted on trial to take less than a full load. I pointed this out to Professor Poggioli, who was kind enough to remove this stipulation.

The rest of my career in the Graduate School and my admission to the Society is a matter of record known to the Senior Fellows.

In connection with this, I hear that I have been charged with misrepresentation by calling myself "professeur." I did indeed use this term under the heading "profession" on my passport application, for absolutely no other reason than that it seemed the simplest way to describe my situation. In that context, the word "professeur" does not mean at all that I would hold this rank in a university, but simply that I earn a living by teaching. I had nothing to gain by calling myself that way and no confusion was possible, since on the same blank I also stated myself as being a Junior Fellow in the Society of Fellows.

(2) I entered the United States on a Belgian passport LA 68916/11516 with an American visa given at Antwerp. This was in May 1948. My status was that of a visitor. Being married to an American citizen, I was allowed to remain here and started naturalization proceedings, going through the normal series of hearings and investigations. When I was interviewed as a candidate for the Society, I was asked when I expected a decision and I stated my belief that it would be in 1954. On September 28th 1954, I was informed by the Department of Immigration that, in order to obtain a permanent status, I would have to exit from the U.S. and re-enter under the sponsorship of my wife. The legal term used is "voluntary departure." I wish to point out that, in order to obtain this

permission which is considered a privilege, one has to establish good moral character. This means that my entire history, here and abroad, was investigated by the Immigration Service and found to be satisfactory. I foresee no difficulties in accomplishing the formalities leading to my reentry and subsequent naturalization.

(3) My father, Hendrik de Man, former Belgian Minister and Chairman of the social-democrat party, is a highly controversial political figure. Because of his attitude under the German occupation, he was sentenced in absentia after the war and died in exile in Switzerland last year. He remains an extremely debatable case and, for reasons that go to the roots of internal Belgian political problems, his name arouses extremely strong feelings at least in some Belgians, apparently still to-day.

I certainly am in no position to pass judgment on him, but I know that his mistakes were made out of a lack of machiavellism and not out of lack of devotion to his ideals. He did what he thought best for his country and his beliefs, and the final evaluation of his acts is a matter of history. One can find his own justification stated in the last two chapters of his autobiography, published last year in Germany under the title *Gegen den Strom*.

I hear now that I myself am being accused of collaboration. In 1940 and 1941 I wrote some literary articles in the newspaper "le Soir" and, like most of the other contributors, I stopped doing so when nazi thought-control did no longer allow freedom of statement. During the rest of the occupation, I did what was the duty of any decent person. After the war, everyone was subjected to a very severe examination of his political behavior, and my name was not a favorable recommendation. In order to obtain a passport, one had not merely to produce a certificate of good conduct, but also a so-called "certificat de civisme," which stated that one was cleared of any collaboration. I could not possibly have come to this country two times, with proper passport and visa, if there had been the slightest reproach against me. To accuse me now, behind my back, of collaboration, and this to persons of a different nation who can not possibly verify and appreciate the facts, is a slanderous attack which leaves me helpless.

(4) In 1945, after the war, I became co-founder, with three partners, of a publishing firm called Hermes, which specialized in the publication of artbooks. I visited this country for the first time in 1947 on behalf of this firm. I left the firm in 1948, when I decided to return to the U.S., but retained the title

of manager which I shared with the three others, in order to assist with whatever contacts I had made in this country. Since 1950 or 51, I have not heard from the firm. This made me assume that things were not going well but, since I had other things on my mind, I did not give it much thought. I now hear, altogether indirectly, that charges are made against me of mismanagement, forgery, etc. I have two statements to make in answer to this:

a. I have never received any notification of charges against me, although my address has always been known in France and in Belgium, where I have not ceased to correspond with several people and even to publish articles. Up to the moment when I was notified that there were restrictions against granting me a regular passport, I never knew that anything was wrong. Up to this very day, and although apparently more has been told to others than to myself, I ignore entirely of what I am accused.

b. I know, in my own conscience, that as long as I was directly connected with the firm, nothing dishonest was done by either myself or my partners. I am not only confident but eager to answer any questions I may be asked about my responsibilities in this matter; as I stated before, this is my main purpose in returning to Belgium immediately. As long as I have not done so, I can offer only this statement to the Society and ask to be given an opportunity to prove it.

I would like to conclude with two general remarks. I think that the way in which this information has been communicated to the Society was calculated, wilfully or not, to cause me a maximum of harm. It made it appear as if I was holding back information about myself which, in fact, I did not possess. It happened entirely without my knowledge, in spite of several personal conversations with the Consul, one, two weeks ago, of nearly an hour which was altogether social and friendly. Also, the content of this information is slanted such as to cause as much damage as possible. The fact that this attitude was certainly not caused by viciousness, but merely by the connotations of my name is hardly a consolation to me.

I have no illusions about the extent of the damage all this has caused me, regardless of what rebuttal I can and will offer. This sudden reflux of a past presented in such a light, when I had devoted the last seven years of my life to building an existence entirely separated from former painful experiences, leaves me weary and exhausted. The only incentive I have to face up to all this, aside of my family, is the strong desire to continue and finish my work. I am certainly in no position to ask the Society of Fellows for anything but a chance to prove the truth of what I have stated in this letter—which means, in very practical terms, the possibility to serve to the end of my first year as a Junior Fellow, letting the future depend on what will happen in Belgium.

I am very grateful for the consideration I have received and the opportunity I was given to justify myself.

Sincerely yours,
[signed]
Paul de Man

[Reprinted from *Responses: On Paul de Man's Wartime Journalism*, edited by Werner Hamacher, Neil Hertz, and Thomas Keenan, by permission of the University of Nebraska Press. Copyright © 1989 by the University of Nebraska Press.]

Appendix B

"The Jews in Contemporary Literature"
Paul de Man

Vulgar anti-Semitism is apt to consider postwar cultural phenomena (after the war of 14–18) as degenerate and decadent because Judaized [*enjuivé*]. Literature hasn't escaped this lapidary judgment: it is enough to have discovered several Jewish writers under Latinized pseudonyms for all contemporary production to be considered polluted and harmful. This conception entails some rather dangerous consequences. In the first place, it condemns a priori an entire literature that in no way deserves this fate. Moreover, from the moment one is inclined to assign some merit to the literature of our day, it would be an unflattering appraisal of Western writers to reduce them to being mere imitators of a Jewish culture that is foreign to them.

The Jews themselves have contributed to the dissemination of this myth. Often, they have glorified themselves as the leaders of the literary movements that characterize our era. But the mistake has, in reality, a deeper cause. The widely held opinion, according to which modern poetry and the modern novel were only monstrous excrescences of the world war, is at the root of the thesis of Jewish dominance. Since the Jews have, in fact, played an important role in the phoney and disordered existence of Europe since 1920, a novel born in that atmosphere would deserve, up to a certain point, the description *enjuivé*.

But the reality is different. It seems that aesthetic evolutions obey very powerful laws that preserve their influence even while humanity is shaken by important events. The world war provoked a profound upheaval in the political and economic world. But artistic life has been disturbed relatively little, and the forms that we know at present are the logical and normal continuation of what preceded them.

This is particularly clear with regard to the novel. Stendhal's definition, according to which "the novel is a mirror which travels along a highway," contains the law that still governs this literary genre today. What was seen as coming first is the obligation to pay scrupulous respect to external reality. But with more profound investigation psychological reality has also been exploited. Stendhal's mirror no longer remains immobile on the road; it undertakes to investigate the most secret corners of the characters' souls. And this domain has proved to be so rich and so fruitful in surprises that it still constitutes the novelist's one and only terrain of investigation.

Gide, Kafka, Hemingway, Lawrence—the list could be extended indefinitely—do nothing but attempt, through methods appropriate to their own personalities, to penetrate the secrets of the interior life. By this shared trait, they reveal themselves, not as innovators breaking with all past traditions, but mere continuators who are only pursuing further the realist aesthetic that is more than a century old.

A similar demonstration can be made in the domain of poetry. The forms that seem most revolutionary to us, such as surrealism and futurism, have, in reality, orthodox ancestors from which they cannot be detached.

One realizes, therefore, that it is absurd to consider contemporary literature as an isolated phenomenon, created by the particular mentality of the 1920s. Likewise, the Jews cannot pretend to have been its creators, or even to have exercised a preponderant influence on its evolution. On close examination, this influence would appear to have extraordinarily little importance, since one might have expected that—given the specific characteristics of the Jewish mind—the latter would have played a more brilliant role in such artistic production. Their cerebralness, their capacity to assimilate doctrines while maintaining a certain cold detachment from them, would seem to be very precious qualities for the work of lucid analysis that the novel requires. But in spite of that, Jewish writers have always remained in the second rank and, to speak only of France, writers on the order of André Maurois, Francis de Croisset, Henri Duvernois, Henri Bernstein, Tristan Bernard, Julien Benda, and so on, are not among the most important figures, and especially not among those who have guided literary genres to some extent. The comparison is, moreover, comforting for Western intellectuals. That they have been able to safeguard themselves from Jewish influence in a domain as culturally representative as literature demonstrates their vitality. We could not have much hope for the future of our civilization if it had let itself be invaded, without resistance, by a foreign force. In keeping its originality and its character intact, despite Semitic interference in all aspects of European life, it has shown that its fundamental nature was healthy. What is more, one can thus see that a solution to the Jewish problem that would envisage the creation of a Jewish colony isolated from Europe would not have regrettable consequences for the literary life of the West. It would lose, in all, some personalities of mediocre worth and would continue, as in the past, to develop according to its higher laws of evolution.

$\mathcal{N}otes$

Introduction

1. Ellen Somekawa and Elizabeth E. Smith, "Theorizing the Writing of History or 'I Can't Think Why It Should Be So Dull, For a Great Deal of It Must Be Invention,'" *Journal of Social History* 22 (Fall 1988): 153.

There is an immense literature on the problem of historical knowledge, on historical objectivity, on the historian's "construction" of the past, and on the very conception of historical reality independent of contemporary discourse. Among recent works that respond to skepticism as to absolute historical truth but reject extreme versions of historical relativism, see Lionel Gossman, *Towards a Rational Historiography* (Philadelphia, 1989); Thomas Haskell, "Objectivity Is Not Neutrality: Rhetoric vs. Practice in Peter Novick's *That Noble Dream*," *History and Theory* 29, no. 2 (1990): 129–57; Carlo Ginzburg, "Checking the Evidence: The Judge and the Historian," *Critical Inquiry* 18 (Autumn 1991); Gabrielle M. Spiegel, "History, Historicism, and the Social Logic of the Text in the Middle Ages," *Speculum* 65 (1990): 59–86; and Joyce Appleby, Lynn Hunt, and Margaret Jacob, *Telling the Truth about History* (New York, 1994).

2. I begin with Sissela Bok's definition of a lie as "any intentionally deceptive message which is *stated*" (Bok, *Lying: Moral Choice in Public and Private Life* [New York, 1978], 13). Andrus Pork refines this definition to distinguish the "direct lie method" from the "blank page method." The former is what we ordinarily think of as simple falsification; the latter, the more complex method, in which verifiable facts are selected and arranged to create an "overall distorted picture" (Pork, "History and Moral Responsibility," *History and Theory* 29, no. 3 [1990]: 322–23).

3. Peter Novick, *That Noble Dream: The "Objectivity Question" and the American Historical Profession* (Cambridge, 1988), 546.

4. Jeffrey Andrew Barash, "Martin Heidegger in the Perspective of the Twentieth Century: Reflections on the Heidegger *Gesamtausgabe*," *Journal of Modern History* 64 (March 1992): 76.

5. Hayden White, *Metahistory: The Historical Imagination in Nineteenth-Century Europe* (New York, 1973; reprint, Baltimore, 1980). I will cite the 1980 edition.

6. *New York Times Book Review*, January 29, 1984, 31. For what might be considered White's minimalist position, not far from conventional standards, see his "Response to Arthur Marwick," *Journal of Contemporary History* 30 (April 1995): 233–46.

7. F. R. Ankersmit, "Reply to Professor Zagorin," *History and Theory* 29, no. 3 (1990): 295–96; Sande Cohen, "Structuralism and the Writing of Intellectual History," *History and Theory* 17, no. 2 (1978): 181.

8. Maurice Mandelbaum, *Philosophy, History and the Sciences: Selected Essays* (Baltimore, 1984), 60.

9. See, for example, Novick, *That Noble Dream*, 278, citing Beard and Becker; Hans-Georg Gadamer, *Truth and Method* (New York, 1986), 483; Barbara Herrnstein-Smith, "Belief and Resistance: A Symmetrical Account," *Critical Inquiry* 18 (Autumn 1991): 130; Barry Barnes, "How Not to Do the Sociology of Knowledge," *Annals of Scholarship: Rethinking Objectivity I* 8, no. 3/4 (1991): 325.

10. Wulf Kansteiner, "Hayden White's Critique of the Writing of History," *History and Theory* 32, no. 3 (1993): 274.

11. Saul Friedlander strikes this chord in Friedlander, ed., *Probing the Limits of Representation: Nazism and the "Final Solution"* (Cambridge, Mass., 1992), 20: "the equivocation of postmodernism concerning 'reality' and 'truth'—that is, ultimately, its fundamental relativism—confronts any discourse about Nazism and the Shoah with considerable difficulties."

12. For a critique of White, see Carlo Ginzburg, "Just One Witness," in Friedlander, *Probing the Limits of Representation*, 82–96.

13. Hayden White, *The Content of the Form: Narrative Discourse and Historical Representation* (Baltimore, 1987), 76–80.

14. Hayden White, "Historical Emplotment and the Problem of Truth," in Friedlander, *Probing the Limits of Representation*, 38. Wulf Kansteiner characterizes White's "attempts to graft the tropological system onto an ontological base and to incorporate the notion of a veto power of historical facts vis-à-vis certain emplotments" as "unsuccessful because they have destabilized his original critique without delineating any consistent new critical position" (Kansteiner, "Hayden White's Critique of the Writing of History," 294). For an essay that does take White beyond the limits he places on skepticism about the historical reality of the Holocaust, see Robert Braun, "The Holocaust and Problems of Historical Representation," *History and Theory* 33, no. 2 (1994): 172–97. Braun feels that "the problematic relation to the referentiality of representation" makes even the views of the Holocaust revisionists, "their bewildering moral and intellectual claims notwithstanding, difficult to deal with" (ibid., 195n).

15. Novick, *That Noble Dream*, 153; Dominick LaCapra, "Rethinking Intellectual History and Reading Texts," in *Modern European Intellectual History: Reappraisals and New Perspectives*, ed. Dominick LaCapra and Steven L. Kaplan (Ithaca, 1982), 80; Joan Wallach Scott, "History in Crisis?: The Others' Side of the Story," *American Historical Review* 94 (June 1989): 690; Allan Megill, "Recounting the Past: 'Description,' Explanation, and Narrative in Historiography," *American Historical Review* 24, no. 3 (June 1989): 653; F. R. Ankersmit, "The Dilemma of Contemporary Anglo-Saxon Philosophy of History," *History and Theory* 24, no. 4, Beiheft 25 (1986): 26. However, Ankersmit believes that these are not "interesting" criteria for distinguishing between satisfactory and unsatisfactory interpretations.

16. Richard Rorty, "Science as Solidarity," in *The Rhetoric of the Human Sciences*, ed.

John S. Nelson, Allan Megill, and Donald N. McCloskey (Madison, 1987), 42. For a discussion of this issue and Rorty's position, see R. P. Peerenboom, "Reasons, Rationales, and Relativisms: What's at Stake in the Conversation over Scientific Rationality?," *Philosophy Today* 34 (Spring 1990): 3–19.

17. Scott, "History in Crisis?," 690. For a discussion of the authority of interpretive communities see Stanley Fish, *Is There a Text in This Class?: The Authority of Interpretive Communities* (Cambridge, Mass., 1980). For a discussion of the relation of T. S. Kuhn's *The Structure of Scientific Revolutions* (Chicago, 1962) to the authority of "historical communities," see David A. Hollinger, "T. S. Kuhn's Theory of Science and Its Implications for History," *American Historical Review* 78, no. 2 (April 1973): 370–93. See also John H. Zammito, "Are We Being Theoretical Yet?: The New Historicism, the New Philosophy of History, and 'Practicing Historians,'" *Journal of Modern History* 65, no. 4 (December 1993): 811–13.

18. Lynn Hunt, "History as Gesture; or, The Scandal of History," in *Consequences of Theory*, ed. Jonathan Arac and Barbara Johnson (Baltimore, 1991), 104.

19. Hunt's appeal to the authority of the discipline more or less overlaps with Megill's "procedural objectivity," which refers to the application of generally accepted procedures without making claims to absolute truth (Megill, "Four Senses of Objectivity," *Annals of Scholarship: Rethinking Objectivity I* 8, no. 3/4 [1991]: 301–20).

20. Ibid., 306.

21. Charles S. Maier, *The Unmasterable Past: History, Holocaust, and German National Identity* (Cambridge, Mass., 1988), 39. Martin Jay writes, "To use Alvin Gouldner's terminology, the 'community of critical discourse' extends beyond any one language group trapped in its own local language genre" (Jay, "Of Plots, Witnesses, and Judgments," in Friedlander, *Probing the Limits of Representation*, 106). For Gouldner's conception see Alvin Gouldner, *The Future of the Intellectuals and the Rise of the New Class: A Frame of Reference, Theses, Conjectures, Arguments, and an Historical Perspective on the Role of Intellectuals and Intelligentsia in the International Class Contest of the Modern Era* (New York, 1979), 28–29.

22. Novick, *That Noble Dream*, 122–28, 301–19.

23. David Hollinger, "Postmodernist Theory and *Wissenschaftliche* Practice," *American Historical Review* 96 (June 1991): 691; Peter Novick, "My Correct Views on Everything," ibid., 701.

24. Richard Rorty, *Philosophy and the Mirror of Nature* (Princeton, 1979), 276, 385.

25. Haskell, "Objectivity Is Not Neutrality," 139.

26. Scott, "History in Crisis?," 681; Somekawa and Smith, "Theorizing the Writing of History," 154.

27. Raymond Martin, "Objectivity and Meaning in Historical Studies: Toward a Post-Analytic View," *History and Theory* 32, no. 1 (1993): 42.

28. For the tip of an immense iceberg, see Michael R. Marrus, *The Holocaust in History* (Hanover, 1987) and "Reflections on the Historiography of the Holocaust,"

Journal of Modern History 66 (March 1994): 92–116; Pierre Vidal-Naquet, *The Assassins of Memory: Essays in the Denial of the Holocaust* (New York, 1992); and Deborah E. Lipstadt, *Denying the Holocaust: The Growing Assault on Truth and Memory* (New York, 1993).

Chapter One

1. Commission of the Central Committee of the C.P.S.U.(B.), ed., *History of the Communist Party of the Soviet Union (Bolsheviks)* (New York, 1939), 346–48.

2. Pierre Vidal-Naquet, "A Paper Eichmann?," *Democracy* (April 1981): 91. The work to which Vidal-Naquet refers is Michael Sayers and Albert E. Kahn, *The Great Conspiracy: The Secret War against Soviet Russia* (Boston, 1946), which now reads as a crude party-line product.

3. For the published transcript of the hearings and the commission's conclusions, see the Preliminary Commission of Inquiry's *The Case of Leon Trotsky: Report of Hearings on the Charges Made against Him in the Moscow Trials* (New York, 1937); and *Not Guilty: Report of the Commission of Inquiry into the Charges Made against Leon Trotsky in the Moscow Trials* (New York, 1937). For useful descriptions of the hearings and the attendant controversy, see James T. Farrell, "Dewey in Mexico," in *John Dewey: Philosopher of Science and Freedom*, ed. Sidney Hook (New York, 1950), 351–77; Sidney Hook, *Out of Step: An Unquiet Life in the Twentieth Century* (New York, 1987), 218–47; Isaac Deutscher, *The Prophet Outcast: Trotsky, 1929–1920* (London, 1963), 371–82; Gary Bullert, *The Politics of John Dewey* (Buffalo, 1983), 134–41; Alan Wald, "Memories of the John Dewey Commission: Forty Years Later," *Antioch Review* 35 (1977): 438–51, and *The New York Intellectuals: The Rise and Decline of the Anti-Stalinist Left from the 1930s to the 1980s* (Chapel Hill, 1987), 128–39; and Robert B. Westbrook, *John Dewey and American Democracy* (Ithaca, 1991), 480–87.

4. Farrell, "Dewey in Mexico," 358n.

5. Hayden White, *Metahistory: The Historical Imagination in Nineteenth-Century Europe* (Baltimore, 1980), 428, 433.

6. Richard Rorty, "Solidarity or Objectivity?," in *Post-Analytic Philosophy*, ed. John Rajchman and Cornel West (New York, 1985), 3–19.

7. Joel Foreman and Richard Rorty, "The Humanities: Asking Better Questions, Doing More Things: An Interview with Richard Rorty," *Federation Review* 7 (March/April 1985): 17. Rorty's point is, "The fact that the Nazis were bad is so clear and evident that I cannot imagine getting more conviction on the subject from one's study in literature, history, or philosophy."

8. Preliminary Commission of Inquiry, *Case of Leon Trotsky*, xv.

9. The Preliminary Commission was actually a subcommittee of the Commission of Inquiry, which also included John R. Chamberlain, Alfred Rosmer, E. A. Ross, Wendelin Thomas, Carlo Tresca, and F. Zamora.

10. "An Open Letter to American Liberals," *Soviet Russia Today*, March 1937, 14–15.

11. Alfred Kazin, *Starting Out in the Thirties* (New York, 1965), 85, 137.

12. *New Republic*, March 17, 1937.

13. Malcolm Cowley, *And I Worked at the Writer's Trade: Chapters of Literary History, 1918–1978* (New York, 1978), 148–52. In 1984 Cowley granted that he "grossly deceived" himself about the trials (Cowley, "Echoes from Moscow: 1937–1938," *Southern Review* 20 [January 1984]: 3).

14. For example, "Behind the Soviet Trials," *Nation*, February 6, 1937.

15. Corliss Lamont, "The Moscow Trials," *Soviet Russia Today*, January 1938, 26.

16. *Soviet Russia Today*, March 1937, 7.

17. Preliminary Commission of Inquiry, *Not Guilty*, 361.

18. Nicholas Rescher and Carey B. Joynt, "Evidence in History and in the Law," *Journal of Philosophy* 66 (June 1959): 561–78.

19. For example, "The Trotsky Commission," *Nation*, May 1, 1937; *New Republic*, March 17, 1937; Selden Redman, "Trotsky in the Kremlin," *Common Sense*, December 1937.

20. Marion Hammett and William Smith, "Inside the Trotsky Trial: A Report by Two Eye-Witnesses," *New Masses*, April 27, 1937, 6–11.

21. See, for example, "Mr. Beals Resigns from Trotsky Commission," *Soviet Russia Today*, May 1937, 38.

22. John A. Britton, *Carleton Beals: A Radical Journalist in Latin America* (Albuquerque, 1987), 166–86. Beals's break with the commission was precipitated by his question as to whether Trotsky had instructed the Soviet agent Borodin to foment revolution in Mexico in the 1920s. This seemed to threaten the security of Trotsky's asylum in Mexico.

23. *New Masses*, April 27, 1937, 6.

24. Ibid., 9.

25. Walter Duranty, "The Riddle of Russia," *New Republic*, July 14, 1937. On Duranty's dubious journalistic career see E. J. Taylor, *Stalin's Apologist: Walter Duranty, The New York Times's Man in Moscow* (New York, 1990); and Malcolm Muggeridge, *Chronicles of Wasted Time: The Green Stick* (New York, 1973), 254–56.

26. The paradigmatic assertion of agnosticism was the analysis of the trial materials by the Yale law professor Fred Rodell, in "Agnosticism in the Moscow Trials," *New Republic*, May 19, 1937.

27. Frank Warren, *Liberals and Communism* (Bloomington, 1966), 185–92.

28. *New Republic*, April 7, 1973, and December 22, 1937.

29. Ibid., December 22, 1937.

30. Frederick L. Schuman, "Leon Trotsky: Martyr or Renegade?," *Southern Review* 3 (1937–38): 51–74.

31. Ibid., 64.

32. Ibid., 68.

33. Ibid., 199–208, published responses by Malcolm Cowley, Max Eastman, John Dewey, Carleton Beals, and James T. Farrell.

34. Sidney Hook, "Liberalism and the Case of Leon Trotsky," *Southern Review* 3

(1937–38): 267–82. This was followed by further correspondence between Hook, Beals, Schuman, and Farrell (pp. 406–16). For a similar debate on the English Left, see Peter Deli, "The Image of the Russian Purges in the *Daily Herald* and the *New States-man*," *Journal of Contemporary History* 20 (April 1985): 261–82; "How They Saw the Moscow Trials," *Survey* 41 (April 1962): 87–95; *New Statesman*, January 30, April 10, and November 6 and 13, 1937; and *Nation*, March 5, 12, and April 23, 1938.

35. *New Republic*, June 2, 1937.

36. "Dewey Rebukes Those 'Liberals' Who Will Not Look into Facts," *New Leader*, May 15, 1937. In his answer to Selden Rodman's piece on Trotsky in *Common Sense*, Dewey wrote, "The question is one of fact, based on one side on the testimony of the Moscow Trials, and on the other side upon the evidence, oral, written and documentary, which the Commission itself gathered" (*Common Sense*, January 1938). In a subsequent critique of Leon Trotsky's "Their Morals and Ours" (*New International*, June 1938, 163–73), Dewey remarks that the means presumably directed to the liberation of mankind "have to be viewed and judged on the ground of their actual objective results" (Dewey, "Means and Ends: Their Interdependence and Leon Trotsky's Essay on 'Their Morals and Ours,'" *The Later Works, 1925–1953* [Urbandale, 1988], 13:351).

37. John Dewey, *Logic, The Theory of Inquiry* (New York, 1938), 287.

38. Richard Rorty, *Objectivity, Relativism, and Truth* (Cambridge, 1994), 65. For an introduction to the controversy over Rorty's Dewey, see Westbrook, *John Dewey and American Democracy*, 539–42.

39. Dewey, *Logic*, 234–39.

40. Ibid., 236–37.

41. Preliminary Commission of Inquiry, *Not Guilty*, 361.

42. Dewey, *Logic*, 231. Ernest Gellner, *Legitimation of Belief* (London, 1974), 31, puts it this way: "For modern philosophy, and its epistemological stress, gain enormously in plausibility when they are read, not as a descriptive or explanatory account of what knowledge 'is really like,' but as a formulation of norms which are to govern and limit our cognitive behavior."

43. David Joravsky, "Soviet Ideology," *Soviet Studies* 18 (1966): 6.

44. In the 1920s Bertrand Russell remarked on the "practical pragmatism" of frame-ups in Russian political trials which the Russian police made every effort to conceal: "This effort after concealment shows that even policemen believe in objective truth in the case of a criminal trial" (*The Will to Doubt* [New York, 1958], 11).

45. People's Commissariat of Justice of the U.S.S.R., *Report of Court Proceedings in the Case of the Anti-Soviet Trotskyite Centre* (Moscow, 1937), 443.

46. William Z. Foster, *Questions and Answers on the Piatakov-Radek Trial* (New York, 1937).

47. Joshua Kunitz, "The Moscow Trial," *New Masses*, March 15, 1938.

48. Maurice Merleau-Ponty, *Humanism and Terror: An Essay on the Communist Problem*, trans. John O'Neill (Boston, 1969).

49. *Workers' Age*, February 20, 1937. See also the issues of February 13, April 24, and

December 18, 1937; and Bertram Wolfe, *New Republic*, June 16 and November 24, 1937.

50. Merleau-Ponty, *Humanism and Terror*, 73.

51. Ibid., 44.

52. Ibid., 53, 103.

53. Raymond Aron, *The Opium of the Intellectuals*, trans. Terence Kilmartin (New York, 1967), 133.

54. Dewey, *Logic*, 237–39.

55. Farrell quoted in Corliss Lamont, ed., *Dialogue on John Dewey* (New York, 1959), 69.

56. Hook, *Out of Step*, 218–19.

Chapter Two

1. Maurice Blanchot, "Les Intellectuels en question: Ébauche d'un réflexion," *Le Débat* 29 (March 1984): 9.

2. Jean-Denis Bredin, *The Affair: The Case of Alfred Dreyfus*, trans. Jeffrey Mehlman (New York, 1986), 280.

3. Robert L. Hoffman, *More Than a Trial: The Struggle over Captain Dreyfus* (New York, 1980), 133–53.

4. It is best to leave that caveat in its context so that there can be no question as to where Bredin does stand:

> If it is thus true that one should be cautious about explaining the Affair summarily as a systematic confrontation between two moralities, a clear division between men of Truth and men of dogma, it is also the case that it revealed in its time and in its way enduring distinctions: on the one hand, those who, in Jaurès's phrase, make of "the human individual the measure of all things, of the country, the family, human property, and God," and on the other, those who posit and serve values higher than the individual: God, the Nation, the Army, the State, the party; those who do battle for Justice, an undefinable ideal of freedom, truth, and generosity, and those who fight on behalf of prejudices, in the etymological sense of the word: the established order, recognized organizations, prior verdicts; those who look toward the ancient cemetery and those who dream of leaping the wall; those taken with memory and those driven by sympathy. (Bredin, *Affair*, 540–41)

5. In 1909, under the pseudonym Henry Dutrait-Crozon, Colonels Georges Louis Larpent and Frédéric Delbecque published *Précis de l'Affaire Dreyfus* (Paris, 1909). Its second edition, which appeared in 1924, became the more or less definitive version of the die-hard affirmation of Dreyfus's guilt. It was reissued in a "revised and augmented" edition as late as 1938. See also their *Joseph Reinach Historien* (Paris, 1905), with a preface by Charles Maurras.

6. Marcel Thomas, *L'Affaire sans Dreyfus* (Paris, 1961).

7. See, for example, the filiopietistic volume of the daughter of Godefroy Cavaignac, the minister of war who bumbled onto the egregious forgery that blew open the case but went to his grave believing that Dreyfus was guilty (Henriette Dardenne-Cavaignac, *Lumières sur l'Affaire Dreyfus* [Paris, 1964]). For strikingly inventive recent contributions, see André Figueras, *Ce Canaille de Dreyfus* (Paris, 1982), and *L'Affaire Dreyfus revue et corrigée* (Paris, 1989).

For a survey and commentary on literature of this sort, see Léon Lipschutz, "Les Fausses légendes de l'Affaire Dreyfus," *Les Cahiers naturalistes* 333 (1967): 73–78.

8. Quoted in Robert Soucy, *Fascism in France: The Case of Maurice Barrès* (Berkeley, 1972), 100. Charles Maurras wrote, "If by chance Dreyfus was innocent, he should have been made a Marshal of France, but a dozen of his principal defenders should have been shot for the triple offense to France, Peace and Reason" (Maurras, *Au Signe de Flore* [Paris, 1931], 55).

9. E. G. Henri Mazel, *Histoire et psychologie de l'Affaire Dreyfus* (Paris, 1934).

10. Brian Chapman, *The Dreyfus Case: A Reassessment* (London, 1955), 360. In the preface of this, the first of two works on the affair, Chapman wrote,

Unhappily much legend is attached to the Affair. To accept the conventional reading of a clerico-military conspiracy is to swallow the propaganda of the Dreyfusards. No conspiracy existed in military circles, none in clerical. The arrest of Déroulède and his allies in August 1899 was no more than the spectacular method of a shaky and nervous Government of rallying opinion to its side. This consideration led me back to a re-examination of the evidence from the beginning. It soon became apparent that much more is to be said for the War Office than has generally been admitted, that anti-Semitism played little, perhaps no, part in the arrest of the unhappy victim or in his trial, that the accusations against the secular Church and, save the Assumptionists, against the religious Orders have the flimsiest foundations. In short, the conventional story is overlaid with propaganda put out by partisans on both sides. (Ibid., 9)

Seventeen years later, in a revised version titled *The Dreyfus Trials* (New York, 1972), Chapman's preface responds to the new material uncovered by Marcel Thomas.

The Dreyfus Case is the classic case of miscarriage of justice: after fifty years we are only just coming to a full understanding of the triviality, the prejudice, the casual cruelty and the clannishness which sent a wholly innocent man to isolation on a bare Caribbean rock, kept him there for five years, and with a lack of scruple and a tenacity worthy of a better cause checked every move to re-open the case. (i)

11. Henri Giscard D'Estaing, *D'Esterhazy à Dreyfus* (Paris, 1950). For the most recent version of this approach, see Jean Doise, *Un Secret bien gardé: Histoire militaire de l'affaire Dreyfus* (Paris, 1944).

12. Douglas Johnson, *France and the Dreyfus Affair* (London, 1966), 5. For a somewhat more qualified, "even-handed" evaluation see Albert S. Lindemann, *The Jew*

Accused: Three Anti-Semitic Affairs (Dreyfus, Belia, Frank) (Cambridge, 1991), 94–128. A recent issue of *l'Histoire*, a journal directed to the general reader, was devoted to "L'Affaire Dreyfus: Vérités et Mensonges" (vol. 173, January 1994). The editors intended to reexamine the affair, as many received opinions were now rejected by historians. The contributors offered some rather ambiguous revisions and many received opinions.

13. Douglas Johnson, *France and the Dreyfus Affair*, 212.

14. Richard Sennett, *The Fall of Public Man* (New York, 1977), 240–51.

15. Richard Griffiths, *The Use of Abuse: The Polemics of the Dreyfus Affair and Its Aftermath* (New York, 1991), 42, 7, 16.

16. Douglas Porch, *The March to the Marne* (Cambridge, 1981), 254.

17. Benjamin Martin, "The Dreyfus Affair and the Corruption of the French Legal System," in *The Dreyfus Affair: Art, Truth and Justice*, ed. Norman L. Kleeblatt (Berkeley, 1987), 37–49.

18. Theodore Zeldin, *The History of France, 1848–1945* (Oxford, 1973), 1:679–82.

19. Charles Péguy, *Notre Jeunesse*, in *Oeuvres en Prose, 1909–1914* (Paris, 1957), 499–653, first published in *Les Cahiers de la Quinzaine*, 12ème cahier de la 11ème série (July 12, 1910).

20. Daniel Halévy, "Apologie pour notre passé," in *Luttes et problèmes* (Paris, 1911), 11–123, first published in *Les Cahiers de la Quinzaine*, 10ème cahier de la 11ème série (April 10, 1910). See the analysis of Alain Silvera, *Daniel Halévy and His Times* (Ithaca, 1966), 100–121.

21. Péguy, *Notre Jeunesse*, 561.

22. Ibid., 643.

23. See, for example, Cécile Delhorbe, *L'Affaire Dreyfus et les écrivains français* (Paris, 1932); Victor Brombert, *The Intellectual Hero: Studies in the French Novel, 1880–1955* (Philadelphia, 1961), 20–40; Stephen Wilson, "Le Monument Henry," *Annales, Économies, Sociétés, Civilizations* 32, no. 2 (March–April 1977): 265–91, and *Ideology and Experience: Anti-Semitism in France at the Time of the Dreyfus Affair* (East Brunswick, N.J., 1982); Christopher Charle, "Champ Littéraire et champ du pouvoir: Les Écrivains et l'Affaire Dreyfus," *Annales, Économies, Sociétés, Civilizations* 32, no. 2 (March–April 1977): 240–64; Madeleine Rebérioux, "Histoire historiens et dreyfusisme," *Revue historique* 518 (April–June 1976): 407–32; H. L. Wesseling, "Reluctant Crusaders: French Intellectuals and the Dreyfus Affair," *Stanford French Review* 1 (Winter 1977): 379–95; *Les Écrivains et l'Affaire Dreyfus*, Actes du colloque organisé par le Centre Charles Péguy et l'Université d'Orléans, 29, 30, 31 Octobre 1981 (Paris, 1983); and Susan Rubin Suleiman, "The Literary Significance of the Dreyfus Affair," in Kleeblatt, *Dreyfus Affair*, 117–39. For the general issue of the "engaged" intellectual, see David Schalk, *The Spectrum of Political Engagement* (Princeton, 1979).

24. Maurice Barrès, *Scènes et doctrines du nationalisme*, in *L'Oeuvre de Maurice Barrès* (Paris, 1966), 5:57.

25. Ferdinand Brunetière, "Après le procès," *Revue des Deux Mondes* 146 (March 15,

1898): 428–46: Maurice Paléologue recalls Brunetière's pugnacious expression of his views in a mixed political gathering:

> And this petition which is being circulated among the "intellectuals." The sole fact that the word "intellectual" has recently been coined for the purpose of setting apart in a kind of exalted social category people who spend their lives in laboratories and libraries points to one of the most absurd eccentricities of our time, namely, the claim that writers, scientists, professors, philologists should be elevated to the rank of supermen. I certainly do not despise intellectual abilities, but their value is only relative. I place will power, force of character, sureness of judgment, practical experience, higher in the social scale. I know farmers and merchants whom I do not hesitate to place far above certain scholars, biologists, and mathematicians whose names I do not care to mention. (*An Intimate Journal of the Dreyfus Case*, trans. Eric Mosbacher [New York, 1957], 113)

26. Émile Durkheim, "Individualism and the Intellectuals," from *Émile Durkheim on Morality and Society*, trans. Mark Traugott (Chicago, 1973), 43–57. First published as "L'Individualisme et les intellectuels," *Revue bleue* 4, no. 10 (1898): 7–13.

27. See Michel Winock, "Le Mythe fondateur: l'affaire Dreyfus," in *Le Modèle republicain*, ed. Serge Bernstein and Odile Rudelle (Paris, 1992), 144; Pierre Birnbaum, "Affaire Dreyfus, culture catholique et antisémitisme," in *Histoire de l'extrême droite en France*, ed. Michel Winock (Paris, 1993), 83–84.

28. Durkheim, "Individualism and the Intellectuals," 50.

29. Ibid.

30. J. P. Honoré, "Autour D'Intellectuel," in *Les Écrivains et l'Affaire Dreyfus*, 152, distinguishes the scientism of the *intellectuels* from that of the nationalists:

> Mais alors que la terminologie scientifique représente, chez les *intellectuels*, l'instrument d'une méthode, elle est chez les nationalistes l'instrument d'une métaphysique: face aux *preuves* de Jaurès, le "nous avons obei à un instinct" de Lemaître est l'argument ultime. [But while scientific terminology represents a methodological tool for the intellectuals, for the nationalists it is a metaphysical instrument: faced with the "proofs" of Jaurès, the "we have followed our instincts" of Lemaître is the ultimate argument.]

31. Brunetière, "Après le procès," 443–44. For Brunetière's critique of the excessive pretensions of the hard sciences, see "Après une viste au Vatican," *Revue des deux mondes* 127 (January 1, 1895): 97–118.

32. Blanchot, "Les Intellectuels en question," 7.

33. Of course, various parties to the polemic were not exempt from academic hubris. J. Psichari, directeur d'études at the École des Hautes Études, suggested that centers of higher education might convoke special assemblies to deliver opinions on important events, thus benefiting from the deliberations of these savants and artistes, whose judgment is essentially disinterested, therefore superior (from a letter to the

Directeur du Temps, reprinted in E. de Haime, *Affaire Dreyfus: Les facts acquis à l'histoire* [Paris, 1898], 298).

34. Émile Duclaux, "Avant le procès," *Le Revue du palais* 5 (May 1, 1898): 241–42. Duclaux's reference to "scientific reasoning" is in the broader European sense of *Wissenschaft*—systematic and disciplined thought not confined to the natural sciences.

35. Arthur Giry, dean of the study of paleography and diplomatics, director of the École des Hautes Études, who provided expert testimony for the Dreyfusards at both trials, would remind the court at Rennes,

Je n'ai besoin de vous dire que, cet examen, je l'ai fait absolument sans parti pris; que j'ai opéré sur ce document sans tenir compte du fond du débat; que j'ai abordé ce problème de l'attribution du bordereau comme je l'aurais fait d'un problème d'histoire. [I don't have to tell you that I have undertaken this analysis completely without parti pris; that I have examined this document without considering the case itself; that I have addressed the question of the attribution of the *bordereau* as I would have handled a historical problem.] (Giry's testimony at the Rennes trial, *Le Procès Dreyfus devant le conseil de guerre de Rennes*, August 7–September 9, 1899 [Paris, 1900], 3:34)

36. Grimaux testimony at the Zola trial, *Le Procès Zola devant la Cour d'Assises de la Seine et la Cour de Cassation (7 Février–23 Février—3 Mars–2 Avril 1898)* (Paris, 1898), 1:534–40.

37. For example, Jules Lemaître, president of La Ligue de la Patrie Française, would assert that the question dividing the French was not "une question de morale: C'est une question de fait" [a moral question but a question of fact]. The point was not to justify the punishment of an innocent man but to know if the ex-captain were innocent or guilty (Lemaître, Première Conférence, "La Patrie Française," January 18, 1899 [Paris, 1899], 5).

38. Pierre Quillard, *Le Monument Henry* (Paris, 1899), 172, includes Léautaud's letter to the *Libre Parole*, which had published the list, edited to read *Pour l'ordre, la justice et la vérité*, insisting on his original version. For Valéry's famous, or infamous, comment, see ibid., 175. Léautaud's recollections were related to Robert Mallet in Paul Léautaud, *Entretiens avec Robert Mallet* (Paris, 1951), 73–75.

39. Allan Megill, *Prophets of Extremity* (Berkeley, 1985), 2.

40. See Martin Jay, " 'The Aesthetic Ideology' as Ideology: or, What Does It Mean to Aestheticize Politics," *Cultural Critique* 21 (Spring 1992): 41–61.

41. Léon Daudet, *Souvenirs des milieux littéraires, politiques, artistiques, et médicaux* (Paris, 1926), 2:47.

42. Marcel Thomas, "Le Cas Valéry," in *Les Écrivains et L'Affaire Dreyfus*, 103–12.

43. Paul Valéry, *Cahiers* (Paris, 1973), 1:129.

44. Blanchot, "Les Intellectuels en question," 13.

45. See, for example, Lucien Goldmann, *Structures mentales et création culturelle* (Paris, 1970), 172.

46. Quoted in Thomas, "Le Cas Valéry," 110.

47. Romain Rolland, quoted in Robert J. Smith, "A Note on Romain Rolland in the Dreyfus Affair," *French Historical Studies* 7 (Fall 1971): 284–87. See also Antoinette Blum, "Romain Rolland face à l'affaire Dreyfus," *Relations internationales* 14 (1978): 127–41; and Suleiman, "Literary Significance of the Dreyfus Affair," 128–29. David James Fisher refers to Romain Rolland's "sanctimonious rationalizations" (*Romain Rolland and the Politics of Intellectual Engagement* [Berkeley, 1988], 20). From the distance of 1940 Rolland recognizes where he should have taken his stand but still more or less conveys his contempt for both camps (Rolland, *Mémoires* [Paris, 1956], 281–95).

48. Blanchot, "Les Intellectuels en question," 16.

49. Georges Sorel, *La Révolution Dreyfusienne* (Paris, 1909), 29–31.

50. Georges Goriely, *Le Pluralisme dramatique de Georges Sorel* (Paris, 1962), 180.

51. Georges Sorel, *Les Illusions du progrès* (Paris, 1921), 276.

52. Shlomo Sand, "Sorel, les Juifs et l'antisémitisme," *Cahiers Georges Sorel* 2 (1984): 7–36.

53. Letter of Sorel to the *Action française*, June 6, 1910, reprinted in Eric Cahm, *Péguy et le nationalisme français de l'Affaire Dreyfus à la grande guerre* (Paris, 1972), 180–81.

54. Sorel, *La Révolution Dreyfusienne*, 57.

55. Charles Maurras, *Au Signe de Flore* (Paris, 1931), 55, 61, 62.

56. Ernest Nolte, *Three Faces of Fascism*, trans. Leila Venneivitz (New York, 1965), 53. See also Michael Curtis, *Three against the Third Republic: Sorel, Barrès, and Maurras* (Princeton, 1959); Soucy, *Fascism in France*; C. Stewart Doty, *From Cultural Rebellion to Counter-Revolution: The Politics of Maurice Barrès* (Athens, Ohio, 1976); and four works by Zeev Sternhell: *Maurice Barrès et le nationalisme français* (Paris, 1972); "Irrationalism and Violence in the French Radical Right: The Case of Maurice Barrès," in *Violence and Aggression in the History of Ideas*, ed. Philip P. Weiner and John Fisher (New Brunswick, 1974); *La Droite révolutionnaire, 1885–1914: les origines françaises du fascisme* (Paris, 1978); and "Le Nationalisme de Barrès," *Les Écrivains et l'Affaire Dreyfus*, 123–35.

57. Léon Blum, *Souvenirs sur l'Affaire* (Paris, 1935), 85–89.

58. Maurice Barrès, *Les Déracinés*, in *L'Oeuvre de Maurice Barrès* (Paris, 1965), 3:26.

59. Maurice Barrès, *Mes Cahiers* (Paris, 1930), 2:86, and *Scènes et doctrines du nationalisme*, 198.

60. Maurice Barrès, *Scènes et doctrines du nationalisme*, 90.

61. Ibid., 52–54.

62. Marcel Proust, *Remembrance of Things Past*, trans. C. K. Scott Moncrief and Terence Kilmartin (New York, 1981), 2:298.

63. Richard Rorty, *Objectivity, Relativism, and Truth* (Cambridge, 1991), 21–45.

64. Barrès, *Scènes et doctrines du nationalisme*, 29–30.

65. Sternhell, "Le Nationalisme de Barrès," 128. On the reactionary nature of the evocation of some essential "French identity," see Herman Lebovics, *True France: The Wars over Cultural Identity, 1900–1945* (Ithaca, 1992), xiii.

66. Ernest Gellner, "The New Idealism," in *Cause and Meaning in the Social Sciences*, ed. Ernest Gellner (London, 1973), 66.

67. In a letter to Péguy, Claudel praised *Notre Jeunesse* but could not share Péguy's sympathy for the Jews or the Dreyfusards: "Votre jugement sur le dreyfusisme serait peut-être différent si comme moi vous l'aviez vu de l'étranger, si vous aviez lu le nom de la France bafoué, insulté avec rage chaque matin dans toutes les langues du monde. Cela m'a suffi. On n'a jamais de faire du mal à sa mère" ["Perhaps your judgment on Dreyfusism would be different if like me you had seen it from abroad, if each morning you had read the name of France ferociously reviled and insulted in every language of the world. One never repudiates his mother"] (quoted in Henri de Lubac and Jean Bastaire, *Claudel et Péguy* [Paris, 1974], 132).

68. Barrès, *Scènes et doctrines du nationalisme*, 47–51; Maurras, *Au Signe de Flore*, 62; Daudet, *Souvenirs*, 2:110.

69. Lucien Herr, "Lettre à Maurice Barrès," in *Choix d'écrits* (Paris, 1932), 1:41.

70. Michael R. Marrus, "'En famille': The Dreyfus Affair and the Myths," *French Politics and Society* 12 (Fall 1994): 77–90.

71. Geoffrey Cubitt, *The Jesuit Myth: Conspiracy Theory and Politics in Nineteenth-Century France* (Oxford, 1993), 175–78.

72. Richard J. Bernstein, "Dewey, Democracy: The Task Ahead of Us," in *Post-Analytic Philosophy*, ed. John Rajchman and Cornel West (New York, 1985), 52.

Chapter Three

1. Perhaps "surprise" should be in quotation marks. Apparently some of de Man's friends and colleagues had heard intimations of his past. The articles in the major Belgian journal *Le Soir* had always been accessible to those interested in the history of occupied Belgium. Several of de Man's surviving coevals well remembered what he had done during the war, and although he had been too young to be a public figure, he was the nephew of Henri de Man, a major national personality.

One is reminded of the nineteenth-century political "surprises" when the tacitly ignored sex lives of a Dilke or a Parnell were publicly exposed.

2. *New York Times*, December 1, 1987.

3. Among other testimonials, see *Yale French Studies* 69 (1985). The issue is entitled "The Lesson of Paul de Man."

4. For the factual outline of his early life and wartime career, see *Responses: On Paul de Man's Wartime Journalism*, ed. Werner Hamacher, Neil Hertz, and Thomas Keenan (Lincoln, 1989).

5. H. de Man's first name is alternately spelled Henri or Hendrik depending on French or Flemish preference. See Dick Pels, "Treason of the Intellectuals: Paul de Man and Hendrik de Man," *Theory, Culture and Society* 8 (1991): 21–56.

6. Werner Hamacher, Neil Hertz, and Thomas Keenan, eds., *Wartime Journalism, 1939–1943, by Paul de Man* (Lincoln, 1988).

7. David Lehman, *Signs of the Times: Deconstruction and the Fall of Paul de Man* (New York, 1991), 212.

8. David Lehman, "Deconstructing de Man's Life," *Newsweek*, February 15, 1988. Mehlman wrote that his views were "somewhat misrepresented in a truncated quotation in the *Newsweek* article," but the general thrust of his piece in *Responses* comes to something like that in his evaluation of the deconstructionist reading of the profascist past of Heidegger, Blanchot, and Derrida (Mehlman, "Perspectives: On de Man and *Le Soir*," in Hamacher, Hertz, and Keenan, *Responses*, 330).

9. Walter Kendrick, "De Man That Got Away: Deconstructors on the Barricades," *Village Voice*, April 12, 1988.

10. Jon Wiener, "Deconstructing de Man," *Nation*, January 9, 1988. For another example of what can only be described as bad history by an indignant historian, see Gerald D. Nash, "Point of View: One Hundred Years of Western History," *Journal of the West* 32 (January 1993): 3–4. Nash says that de Man was a "virulent supporter of the Nazis in the 1930s" (simply wrong: de Man belonged to a student group on the democratic Left) and that Geoffrey Hartman defended de Man (which he did) and de Man's "totalitarian ideology" (which is ludicrous).

11. *Nation*, April 9, 1988; Jon Wiener, "The Responsibilities of Friendship: Jacques Derrida on Paul de Man's Collaboration," *Critical Inquiry* 15 (Summer 1989): 797–803.

12. Jacques Derrida, "Like the Sound of the Sea Deep within a Shell: Paul de Man's War," *Critical Inquiry* 14 (Spring 1988): 590–652; "On Jacques Derrida's 'Paul de Man's War,'" *Critical Inquiry* 15 (Summer 1989): 765–873.

13. James Atlas, "The Case of Paul de Man," *New York Times Magazine* (August 28, 1988).

14. Cornel West, "Theory, Pragmatism, and Politics," in *Consequences of Theory*, ed. Jonathan Arac and Barbara Johnson (Baltimore, 1991), 29.

15. J. Hillis Miller, "An Open Letter to Professor Jon Wiener," in Hamacher, Hertz, and Keenan, *Responses*, 342.

16. Roger Kimball, "Professor Hartman Reconstructs Paul de Man," *New Criterion* (May 1988): 37. Kimball is referring to Hartman's "Paul de Man, Fascism, and Deconstruction," *New Republic*, March 7, 1988.

17. Joan W. Scott, "The Evidence of Experience," *Critical Inquiry* 17 (Summer 1991): 783.

18. "There are few more pernicious beliefs than the one which suggests that we have cast serious doubts upon a belief by explaining why someone came to hold it" (Arthur C. Danto, *Narration and Knowledge* [New York, 1985], 98).

19. Jonathan Culler, "It's Time to Set the Record Straight about Paul de Man and His Wartime Articles for a Pro-Fascist Newspaper," *Chronicle of Higher Education*, July 13, 1989, section 2; Christopher Norris, "Paul de Man's Past," *London Review of Books*, February 4, 1988, 7; J. Hillis Miller, Guest Column, *Times Literary Supplement*, June 17–23, 1988, 676.

20. Jonathan Culler, "'Paul de Man's War' and the Aesthetic Ideology," *Critical Inquiry* 15 (Summer 1989): 777–83.

21. *London Review of Books*, March 17 and April 21, 1988.

22. Christopher Norris, *Paul de Man: Deconstruction and the Critique of Aesthetic Ideology* (New York, 1988), 177–211.

23. Miller, *Times Literary Supplement*, June 17–23, 1988, 676, 685, and "An Open Letter to Jon Wiener," 334–42.

24. Pauline Marie Rosenau, *Post-Modernism and the Social Sciences: Insights, Inroads, and Intrusions* (Princeton, 1992), 119. Her citations are to J. Hillis Miller, "The Disarticulation of the Self in Nietzsche," *The Monist* 64 (April 1981): 247–61; Jonathan Culler, *On Deconstruction: Theory and Criticism after Structuralism* (New York, 1982); and Christopher Norris, *Deconstruction and the Interests of Theory* (London, 1988).

25. Lehman, *Signs of the Times*, 257, commenting on Jacques Derrida. See, for example, Patrick Parrinder's harsh comment on Miller's attacks on "falsifications, distortions," and so forth: "Has he forgotten that the customary oppositions of truth and error, of referentiality and non-referentiality, of interpretation and misinterpretation, and of fact and fiction have been constantly 'called into question' (and as often as not declared illusory) in his own writings and those of his admirers?" (Parrinder, *Times Literary Supplement*, June 24–30, 1988).

Steven Shaviro has remarked on another discrepancy: "the degree to which Paul de Man has been idealized and fetishized by his followers: idealized, it would seem, to the very extent that he always warned against the dangers of idealization" ("Complicity and Forgetting," *Modern Language Notes* 105 [September 1990]: 821).

26. Terry Eagleton, "The Emptying of a Former Self," *Times Literary Supplement*, May 26–June 1, 1989, 573–74.

27. Gerald Graff, "Looking Past the de Man Case," in Hamacher, Hertz, and Keenan, *Responses*, 249.

28. Louis O. Mink, "Philosophy and Theory of History," in *International Handbook of Historical Studies: Contemporary Research and Theory*, ed. George G. Iggers and Harold T. Parker (Westport, 1979), 25.

29. Norris, "Paul de Man's Past," 7.

30. The page of the March 4, 1941, issue of *Le Soir* on which de Man's article appeared is reproduced in Hamacher, Hertz, and Keenan, *Wartime Journalism, 1939–1943*, 286–92; his article is also reproduced (ibid., 45). Because this article is a central text for conflicting evaluations of de Man's behavior, it is presented in Appendix B.

31. De Man, "People and Books: A View on Contemporary German Fiction," *Het Vlaamsche Land*, August 20, 1942, 325–26.

32. At least as quoted by Wiener in his *Nation* article. For a fair and balanced survey of de Man's favorable reviews of works by French and Belgian collaborationists, "realists," and fascists by a former student of de Man, see Alice Yaeger Kaplan, "Paul de Man, *Le Soir*, and the Francophone Collaboration (1940–1942)," in Hamacher, Hertz, and Keenan, *Responses*, 266–84.

33. This is reproduced with slight changes in Hamacher, Hertz, and Keenan, *Responses*, 127–64. My citations are from the *Critical Inquiry* version. Derrida refers to the phone call from *Critical Inquiry* which proposed that he be the first to speak ("Like the Sound of the Sea," 596).

34. Mark Edmundson, "A Will to Cultural Power: Deconstructing the de Man Scandal," *Harper's* 277 (July 1988): 67–71.

35. Norris, *Paul de Man*, 211; Walter Kendrick, "Blindness and Hindsight: Dispatches from the de Man Front," *Village Voice Literary Supplement*, October 1988.

36. For a rather oblique defense of Derrida against this criticism, see Bryan D. Palmer, *Descent into Discourse: The Reification of Language and the Writing of Social History* (Philadelphia, 1990), 277.

37. Derrida, "Like the Sound of the Sea," 594.

38. Ibid., 604–6.

39. Ibid., 600.

40. Ibid., 638.

41. Ibid., 607.

42. Derrida, "Biodegradables: Seven Diary Fragments," *Critical Inquiry* 15 (Summer 1989): 812–73.

43. Derrida, "Like the Sound of the Sea," 621–32.

44. De Man, "*Voir la Figure* de Jacques Chardonne," *Le Soir*, October 28, 1941; Hamacher, Hertz, and Keenan, *Wartime Journalism, 1939–1943*, 158–59.

45. Derrida, "Like the Sound of the Sea," 613. Littré does not list "sharp" as one of the meanings of *netteté*, but it is sometimes used, as in a "sharp" image, which is not the same as a sharp edge.

46. Ibid., 651.

47. Thomas Fries, "Paul de Man's 1940–1942 Articles in Context," in Hamacher, Hertz, and Keenan, *Responses*, 197–98.

48. Ian Balfour, "'Difficult Reading': De Man's Itineraries," in Hamacher, Hertz, and Keenan, *Responses*, 8–9. Like many other commentators, Balfour concedes an extremely damaging "on the one hand": "Gestures such as de Man's praise of Péguy and the denigration of Brasillach and the other Nazi ideologues for their bad political judgment cannot undo all the damage done by the disturbing articles, indeed by their very forum regardless of their content."

49. Peggy Kamuf, "Impositions: A Violent Dawn at *Le Soir*," in Hamacher, Hertz, and Keenan, *Responses*, 264.

50. Ortwin de Graef, "Aspects of the Context of Paul de Man's Earliest Publications *followed by* Notes on Paul de Man's Flemish Writings," in Hamacher, Hertz, and Keenan, *Responses*, 96–126. In a subsequent publication de Graef finds a motive for de Man's collaborationism in a sort of misplaced scientism, an insight that "allows us to address this collaboration along lines that are less overdetermined by the rhetoric of outright denunciation or circuitous exculpation" (De Graef, *Serenity in Crisis: A Preface*

to *Paul de Man, 1939–1960* [Lincoln, 1993], 13). "Circuitous exculpation" perfectly characterizes de Graef's contribution to *Responses*.

51. Kaplan, "Paul de Man, *Le Soir*, and the Francophone Collaboration," 282; David Carroll, "The Temptation of Fascism and the Question of Literature: Justice, Sorrow, and Political Error (An Open Letter to Jacques Derrida)," *Cultural Critique* 15 (Spring 1990): 72.

52. Lucien Rebatet, *Les Décombres* (Paris, 1942), 566. For a description of Rebatet and the bowdlerization of later issues of the 1942 work, see Alice Yaeger Kaplan, *Reproduction of Banality: Fascism, Literature, and French Intellectual Life* (Minneapolis, 1986), 125–41. See also Robert Belot, *Lucien Rebatet: Un itinéraire fasciste* (Paris, 1994), 282–301.

53. Dennis Donoghue, "The Strange Case of Paul de Man," *New York Review of Books*, June 29, 1989, 34.

54. Geoffrey Hartman, "History and Judgment: The Case of Paul de Man," *History and Memory* 1 (1988): 63. Hartman does not extend this argument to the anti-Semitic passages, which he cannot extenuate.

55. Derrida, "Like the Sound of the Sea," 631, 642, 648.

56. Marjorie Perloff, "Response to Jacques Derrida," *Critical Inquiry* 15 (Summer 1989): 774. "In some cases positive testimony is highlighted and damaging testimony simply omitted. Several people cite the testimony of George Goriely, a Jewish friend of de Man, who recalled no trace of racism and the covert assistance of various Jews during the war, while neglecting to quote Goriely's description of de Man as 'completely, almost pathologically dishonest. . . . Swindling, forging, lying were, at least at the time, second nature to him'" (ibid.).

Steven Shaviro wonders what "special dispensation" allowed Derrida and Miller "to single out de Man's text from all the other antisemitic writing being produced in Europe at the time" for "all the patience, sympathy, suspension of judgment, and sensitivity to possible ambiguities at our disposal" (Shaviro, "Complicity and Forgetting," 822).

57. Rodolphe Gasché, "Edges of Understanding," in Hamacher, Hertz, and Keenan, *Responses*, 210. "To read here, means to attentively seek to understand the sense of the writings in question which also implies situating them in their proper context, a skill normally expected from educated persons, but nowadays often associated with deconstruction, especially if the sense of the written does not fit preconceived notions."

58. De Graef, *Serenity in Crisis*, 101.

59. *Economist*, May 18–24, 1991, 95; Jacob Neusner, "Anti-Semitism: No Ifs or Buts," *Jewish Advocate*, March 31, 1988, section 2, p. 2.

60. See, with special reference to French writers, Gérard Loiseaux, *La Littérature de la défaite et de la collaboration* (Paris, 1984); Pascal Fouché, *L'Edition française sous l'Occupation, 1940–1944* (Paris, 1987); Pierre Assouline, *Gaston Gallimard: A Half-Century of French*

Publishing, trans. Harold J. Samuelson (New York, 1988); Claude Lévy, "La Presse de Collaboration en France occupée: Conditions d'existence," *Revue d'histoire de la deuxième guerre mondiale* 80 (October 1980): 87–100; and Robert Pickering, "The Implications of Legalised Publication," in *Collaboration in France: Politics and Culture during the Nazi Occupation, 1940–1944*, ed. Gerhard Herschfeld and Patrick Marsh (Oxford, 1989), 162–89.

61. Zeev Sternhell, "The Making of a Propagandist," *New Republic*, March 6, 1989, 31.

62. Andrej Warminski, "Terrible Reading (preceded by 'Epigraphs')," in Hamacher, Hertz, and Keenan, *Responses*, 388.

63. Edouard Colinet, "Paul de Man and the *Cercle du libre examen*," in Hamacher, Hertz, and Keenan, *Responses*, 426.

64. Ernesto Laclau, "Totalitarianism and Moral Indignation," *Diacritics* 20 (Fall 1990): 88. "All witnesses," including some of de Man's defenders, do not agree.

65. Jean Stengers, "Paul de Man, a Collaborator?" in *(Dis)continuities: Essays on Paul de Man*, ed. Luc Herman, Kris Hambeede, and Geert Lernout (Amsterdam, 1989), 43–50.

66. William Flesch, "Ancestral Voices: De Man and His Defenders," in Hamacher, Hertz, and Keenan, *Responses*, 175.

67. Carroll, "The Temptation of Fascism," 49.

68. W. Wolfgang Holdheim, "Jacques Derrida's Apologia," *Critical Inquiry* 15 (Summer 1989): 790.

69. Derrida, "Like the Sound of the Sea," 623, 630.

70. Timothy Bahti, "Telephonic Crossroads: The Reversal and the Double Cross," in Hamacher, Hertz, and Keenan, *Responses*, 3, contrasts de Man's article on the Jews with an essay he wrote in the *Cahiers du Libre Examen* and suggests "that the later article ["Les Juifs dans la littérature actuelle"] is specifically an ironic rewriting and rereading of the first ["Le roman anglais contemporain"] would probably have been known by de Man's friends from *Les Cahiers du Libre Examen*." It seems unlikely that de Man's friends from the *Cahiers* who participated in the Belgian Resistance would have picked up that point.

71. Colinet, "Paul de Man and the *Cercle du Libre Examen*," 433; Stengers, "Paul de Man," 43, 49.

72. For the German policy toward the Belgian press, see Else de Bens, "Paul de Man and the Collaborationist Press," in Hamacher, Hertz, and Keenan, *Responses*, 85–95; de Bens, "La Presse au Temps de l'Occupation de la Belgique," *Revue d'histoire de la deuxième guerre mondiale* 80 (October 1970): 1–28.

73. Sternhell, "Making of a Propagandist," 33.

74. Flesch, "Ancestral Voices," 177–78.

75. William P. Ugeux, "The Press under the Occupation," in *Belgium under Occupation*, ed. and trans. Jan-Albert Goris (New York, 1947), 125.

76. Zeev Sternhell, *Neither Right nor Left: Fascist Ideology in France* (Berkeley, 1986), xiii; Loiseaux, *La Littérature de la défaite*, 500.

77. Sandor Goodhart, "Disfiguring de Man: Literature, History and Collaboration," in Hamacher, Hertz, and Keenan, *Responses*, 228.

78. Quoted in David Littlejohn, *The Patriotic Traitors: The History of Collaboration in German-Occupied Europe, 1940–1945* (New York, 1972), 170.

79. In a sympathetic review of Alfred Fabre-Luce, "Journal de la France," *Le Soir*, July 21, 1942, in *Wartime Writings*, 253. De Man is summarizing Fabre-Luce, but it is difficult to read this passage as if de Man did not agree with an argument, "meticulously aligning itself on necessities inscribed in the facts."

80. For example, see Shoshana Felman, "Paul de Man's Silence," *Critical Inquiry* 15 (Summer 1989): 704–44.

81. Samuel Weber, "The Movement Disfigured," in Hamacher, Hertz, and Keenan, *Responses*, 404. See Kenneth Asher, "The Moral Blindness of Paul de Man," *Telos* 82 (Winter 1989–1990): 197–205, who characterizes the passage from Weber as "unintentional parody."

82. Warminski, "Terrible Reading," 392.

83. Derrida, "Biodegradables," 823, 827.

84. Gasché, "Edges of Understanding," 209.

85. De Graef, *Serenity in Crisis*, 119.

86. Artis Feoretos, "To Read Paul de Man," in De Graef, *Serenity in Crisis*, 171.

87. Hans-Jost Frey, "Literature, Ideology," in Hamacher, Hertz, and Keenan, *Responses*, 192.

88. Hartman, "History and Judgment," 64–67; Barbara Johnson, *A World of Difference* (Baltimore, paperback edition, 1989), xv–xvi.

89. Gasché, "Edges of Understanding," 215. See also Deborah Esch, "The Work to Come," *Diacritics* 20 (Fall 1990): 41.

Shoshana Felman finds the conceptual flaw in de Man's "historical misreading" ("Paul de Man's Silence," 737); Werner Hamacher, in his "hegemonic realism" ("Journals, Politics," in Hamacher, Hertz, and Keenan, *Responses*, 462); Ortwin de Graef, in his scientistic objectivity (*Serenity in Crisis*, 13–14); Geoffrey Hartman, in his "teleological idea of history" ("History and Judgment," 73). Perhaps the most popular flaw is a sinister "aestheticism," to whose deconstruction de Man will allegedly devote the rest of his life.

90. Hamacher, Hertz, and Keenan, *Wartime Journalism, 1939–1943*, 13–14. This is mistakenly dated 1939 in the volume. Miller and Culler present the prewar stand as if it neutralized the wartime collaborationism.

91. Ibid., 66.

92. Ortwin de Graef and Jacques Derrida do see this as a "puzzling" problem. De Graef solves this with reference to de Man's prewar neutralism as continuous with his "Belgicist" line during the occupation; and Derrida finds unfortunate anticipation of

his wartime aberrations in his call for a "new order" in the *Libre Examen* (de Graef, "Aspects of the Context of Paul de Man's Earliest Publications"; Derrida, "Like the Sound of the Sea," 602–3). The language to which Derrida refers was also that of the French Resistance from the Communists to De Gaulle.

93. The letter is reprinted in Hamacher, Hertz, and Keenan, *Responses*, 475–77.

94. Hartman, "History and Judgment," 78.

95. When J. Hillis Miller sets the record straight he cites the date when de Man left *Le Soir*—November 1942—as if that was what de Man had indicated in his letter to the Society of Fellows (Miller, *Times Literary Supplement*, June 17–23, 1988, 685).

96. Paul Morrison, "Paul de Man: Resistance and Collaboration," *Representations* 32 (Fall 1990): 71.

97. The puzzled response to this reference reminded me that I stand on the aged edge of the generation gap. Kirsten Flagstad, the great Wagnerian soprano, had been accused (perhaps incorrectly) of sharing the politics of her husband, a Norwegian collaborationist.

98. James T. Kloppenberg, "Objectivity and Historicism: A Century of American Historical Writing," *American Historical Review* 94 (October 1989): 1030.

99. Morrison, "Paul de Man," 71–72.

100. Russell A. Berman, "Troping to Pretoria: The Rise and Fall of Deconstruction," *Telos* 85 (Fall 1990): 15–16.

101. Eagleton, "Emptying of a Former Self," 573–74.

102. Louis Menand, "The Politics of Deconstruction," *New York Review of Books*, November 21, 1991, 39–44.

103. Dominick LaCapra, "The Personal, The Political and the Textual: Paul de Man as Object of Transference," *History and Memory* 4 (Spring–Summer 1992): 30.

104. Jameson's remarks on the controversy appear in Frederic Jameson, *Postmodernism, or the Cultural Logic of Late Capitalism* (Durham, 1991), 256. They have also been criticized in "Forum: Martin Jay and Jane Flax," *History and Theory* 32, no. 3 (1993): 296–304.

105. Shoshana Felman remarks that the intersections of her conclusions with those of Ortwin de Graef, independently arrived at, "bear uncanny witness to the accuracy of the paths we have both chosen in de Man's text." As if there were no such thing as error squared (Felman, "Paul de Man's Silence," 730n).

Chapter Four

1. The substance of the story can be pieced together from "Remarks of President Reagan to Regional Editors," White House, April 18, 1985; "Remarks of President Reagan at Bergen-Belsen Concentration Camp," May 5, 1985; and "Remarks of President Reagan at Bitburg Air Base," May 5, 1985, quoted in Geoffrey H. Hartman, ed., *Bitburg in Moral and Political Perspective* (Bloomington, Ind., 1986), 239–40, 253–55, 258–61.

2. *New York Times*, May 5, 1985, and *Time*, May 20, 1985, quoted in Hartman, *Bitburg in Moral and Political Perspective*, 175, 179.

3. Ronald Reagan, *Public Papers of the President of the United States. 1985, Book I* (Washington, 1988), 330–31.

4. Interview with Lou Cannon, Dave Hoffman, and Lynn Downie of the *Washington Post*, ibid., 383. That was on April 1. On April 18, in a question-and-answer session with regional broadcasters, it came out like this: "and all of this when most of the people in Germany today weren't alive or were very small children when this was happening" (ibid., 457).

5. George P. Shultz, *Turmoil and Triumph: My Years as Secretary of State* (New York, 1993), 541.

6. David Carr, "Narrative and the Real World: An Argument for Continuity," *History and Theory* 24, no. 2 (1986): 120. Carr summarizes a current of thought he wishes to criticize.

7. Louis Mink, "Narrative Form as a Cognitive Instrument," in *The Writing of History: Literary Form and Historical Understanding*, ed. Robert H. Canary and Henry Kozicki (Madison, 1978), 145; Richard McGuire, "Narrative Persuasion in Rhetorical Theory," in *On Narrative*, ed. Helmut Geissner (Frankfurt am Main, 1987), 165. And see Philip Abrams, *Historical Sociology* (Ithaca, 1892): "An essential feature of narrative would seem to be its ability both to carry analysis and to protect analysis from the sorts of critical reading appropriate to it" (309).

8. Jerome Bruner, "The Narrative Construction of Reality," *Critical Inquiry* 18 (Autumn 1991): 4–5.

9. Sidney Blumenthal, *Our Long National Daydream: A Political Pageant of the Reagan Era* (New York, 1988), 3–9. See also Michael Rogin, *Ronald Reagan, The Movie, and Other Episodes in Political Demonology* (Berkeley, 1987), xvi.

10. Paul Ricoeur, *Hermeneutics and the Human Sciences: Essays on Language, Action, and Interpretation* (Cambridge, 1981), 289. However, Ricoeur wishes to emphasize that

> however fictional the historical text may be, it claims nevertheless to be a representation *of* reality. In other words, history is both a literary *artefact* (and in this sense a fiction) and a representation of *reality*. It is a literary artefact insofar as, in the manner of all literary texts, it tends to assume the status of a self-sufficient system of symbols. It is a representation of reality insofar as the world that it depicts—and which is the "world of the work"—claims to hold for real events in the real world. (Ibid., 291)

11. Mink, "Narrative Form as a Cognitive Instrument," 144.

12. Hayden White, *Metaphysics* (Baltimore, 1980), 9; see also Hayden White, "The Historical Text as Literary Artifact," in Canary and Kozicki, *Writing of History*, 48, where he observes that it would be "inappropriate" to emplot President Kennedy's assassination as a comedy.

13. *The Washington Post*, May 6, 1985, quoted in Hartman, *Bitburg in Moral and Political Perspective*, 178.

14. Hartman, *Bitburg in Moral and Political Perspective*, 8.

15. Hartman, "Meaning, Error, Text," *Yale French Studies* 69 (1985): 146.

16. Russell Berman, "Troping to Praetoria: The Rise and Fall of Deconstruction," *Telos* 85 (Fall 1990): 8. See also Tobin Siebers, *Cold War Criticism and the Politics of Skepticism* (New York, 1993), 144n.

17. Sally Haslanger, "On Being Objective and Being Objectified," in *A Mind of One's Own: Feminist Essays on Reason and Objectivity*, ed. Louise M. Antony and Charlotte Witt (Boulder, 1993), 8. Haslanger is not affirming this view but summarizing it.

18. One commentator on presidential rhetoric has identified Reagan's style as "effeminate," ideally suited to the medium of television (Kathleen Hall Jamieson, *Eloquence in an Electronic Age: The Transformation of Political Speechmaking* [New York, 1988], 81–89).

19. Since I first wrote these lines, subjects even more exempt from rationality have come into public view out there in militia country.

20. Sidney Hook, *Out of Step: An Unquiet Life in the Twentieth Century* (New York, 1988), 454–55.

21. David Wise, *The Politics of Lying: Government Deception, Secrecy, and Power* (New York, 1973).

22. Arthur Sylvester, "The Government Has the Right to Lie," *Saturday Evening Post*, November 18, 1973, 14–16.

23. *The Pentagon Papers: The Senator Gravel Edition* (Boston, 1971), 1:571, 573–83, xii.

24. For examples from another regime see Richard Reeves, *President Kennedy: Profile of Power* (New York, 1993).

25. Mark Green and Gail MacColl, *There He Goes Again: Ronald Reagan's Reign of Error* (New York, 1983), 8–9.

26. Mark Green and Gail MacColl, *Reagan's Reign of Error: The Instant Nostalgia Edition* (New York, 1987).

27. Alexander Cockburn, *Corruptions of Empire: Life and the Reagan Era* (London/New York, 1987), 346.

28. Green and MacColl, *Reagan's Reign of Error*, 125; see also Rogin, *Ronald Reagan, The Movie*.

29. George Shultz recalls that Reagan had never said he visited the camps but that his remarks were garbled in translation (Shultz, *Turmoil and Triumph*, 551). However, Garry Wills cites evidence indicating that Simon Wiesenthal and Rabbi Hier of the Wiesenthal Center thought that the president had told them the same story on another occasion. It is difficult to believe that the translation was garbled both times around (Wills, *Reagan's America: Innocents at Home* [New York, 1987], 168–69). See also Lou Cannon, *President Reagan: The Role of a Lifetime* (New York, 1991), 486–90.

30. Sissela Bok, *Lying: Moral Choice in Public and Private Life* (New York, 1978), 16–17.

31. Ronald Reagan, *Public Papers of the Presidents of the United States, Book 2* (Washington, 1989), 1570, 1572, 1575; Larry Speakes with Robert Pack, *Speaking Out: The Reagan Presidency from Inside the White House* (New York, 1988), 292–94.

32. Paul K. Conkin, "Review Essay," *History and Theory* 29, no. 2 (1990): 230. Conkin does grant authority to logical inference from what he calls "surviving artifacts." See also Robert Braun, "The Holocaust and Problems of Historical Representation," *History and Theory* 33, no. 2 (1994): 197.

33. Edwin Meese, *With Reagan: The Inside Story* (Washington, 1992), 26.

34. Lyn Nofziger, *Nofziger* (Washington, 1992), 285.

35. Donald T. Regan, *For the Record* (New York, 1988), 249–50.

36. Shultz, *Turmoil and Triumph*, 819.

37. Michael K. Deaver, *Behind the Scenes* (New York, 1987), 77–80, 177.

38. Peggy Noonan, *What I Saw at the Revolution: A Political Life in the Reagan Era* (New York, 1990), 141–42, 184–85.

39. Cannon, *President Reagan*, 138.

40. William F. Lewis, "Telling America's Story: Narrative Form and the Reagan Presidency," *Quarterly Journal of Speech* 73 (August 1987): 281, 282, 283, 289–90.

41. Dilys M. Hill and Phil Williams, *The Reagan Presidency: An Incomplete Revolution?* (Hampshire and London, 1990), 234.

42. See, for example, David Mervin, "The Competence of Ronald Reagan," *Parliamentary Affairs* 40 (April 1987): 203–17; Haynes Johnson, *Sleepwalking through History: America in the Reagan Years* (New York, 1991), 455.

43. Robert Hughes, *Culture of Complaint: The Fraying of America* (New York, 1993), 41. See also David Bromwich, *Politics by Other Means* (New Haven, 1992), 225, who refers to "President Reagan's great work" as "the education of a whole society down to his level."

44. Diane Rubenstein, "The Mirror of Reproduction: Baudrillard and Reagan's America," *Political Theory* 17 (November 1989): 586, 587, 597. See also William Chaloupka, *Knowing Nukes: The Politics and Culture of the Atom* (Minneapolis, 1992), 97.

45. Umberto Eco, *Travels in Hyper Reality* (New York, 1983), 7; Jean Baudrillard, *America* (New York, 1988), 101, 118. For a similar view in less apodictic language see Ada Louise Huxtable, "Inventing American Reality," *New York Review of Books*, December 3, 1992.

46. For example, James Combs, *The Reagan Range: The Nostalgic Myth in American Politics* (Bowling Green, 1993); Richard Slotkin, *Gunfighter Nation: The Myth of the Frontier in Twentieth-Century America* (New York, 1992), 644–45.

47. Rubenstein, "Mirror of Reproduction," 599.

48. Shultz, *Turmoil and Triumph*, 54.

49. Midge Decter, "Bitburg: Who Forgot What," *Commentary*, August 1985.

50. Midge Decter, "Ronald Reagan and the Cultural War," *Commentary*, March 1991.

51. Hughes, *Culture of Complaint*, 27.

52. Dinesh D'Souza, *Illiberal Education: The Politics of Race and Sex on Campus* (New York, 1990).

53. Gertrude Himmelfarb, *On Looking into the Abyss: Untimely Thoughts on Culture and Society* (New York, 1994), xii.

54. Martin Anderson, *Impostors in the Temple* (New York, 1992), 149.

55. Martin Anderson, *Revolution* (New York, 1988). For Anderson's "spin control" in service of the future president, see "Challenges to Statements Put Reagan on the Defensive," *New York Times*, April 13, 1980.

56. William J. Bennett, *To Retain a Legacy: A Report on the Humanities in Higher Education* (Washington, 1984), 16.

57. William J. Bennett, *The De-Valuing of America: The Fight for Our Culture and Our Children* (New York, 1992), 29, 246. On the disjunction between Bennett's, and George Will's, perspective "inside the school gates" and their acceptance of Ronald Reagan and "the culture he represents," see Bromwich, *Politics by Other Means*, 83–97.

58. Reagan, *Public Papers of the Presidents, Book 1* (Washington, 1987), 209.

59. Lynne V. Cheney, *Telling the Truth* (Washington, 1992), 20.

60. George F. Will, "Literary Politics," *Newsweek*, April 22, 1991.

61. George F. Will, *Suddenly: The American Ideal Abroad and at Home, 1986–1990* (New York, 1990), 149–50.

62. Alan Ryan, "A Plague on Both Houses," *TLS*, May 21, 1993.

Conclusion

1. Hilary Putnam, *Reason, Truth, and History* (Cambridge, 1993), 49.

2. Donald Davidson, "On the Very Idea of a Conceptual Scheme," in *Post-Analytic Philosophy*, ed. John Rajchman and Cornel West (New York, 1985), 142.

3. Joan Scott, "The Evidence of Experience," *Critical Inquiry* 17 (Summer 1991): 791.

4. Following Karl Popper, Ernest Gellner characterizes this familiar polemical maneuver as the "myth of the framework": "The myth of the framework has indeed become the last refuge of scoundrels. The idea that we are all of us, prisoners of our 'framework,' enables them to discount ideas of their opponents, and to stick to their own without seriously examining either" (Gellner, *Legitimation of Belief* [Cambridge, 1974], 182).

5. Hayden White, "The Politics of Historical Interpretation," in *The Content of the Form: Narrative Discourse and Historical Representation* (Baltimore, 1987), 74–75.

6. Carlo Ginzburg, "Just One Witness," in Saul Friedlander, *Probing the Limits of Representation: Nazism and the "Final Solution"* (Cambridge, Mass., 1992), 93.

7. Joyce Appleby, Lynn Hunt, and Margaret Jacob, *Telling the Truth about History* (New York, 1994), 269.

8. Ibid., 283–91.

9. Michael Roth, "Unsettling the Past: Objectivity, Irony, and History," *Annals of Scholarship* 9, no. 2 (1992): 179–80.

10. Appleby, Hunt, and Jacob, *Telling the Truth about History*, 286.

Index

New York Herald-Tribune, 24

New York Times, 7, 24, 62, 97, 98, 102, 109

New York Times Book Review, 3

New York Times Magazine, 65

Nicaragua, 105, 112

Nofziger, Lyn, 108

Nolte, Ernst, 55

Noonan, Peggy, 109, 110; What I Saw at the Revolution, 109

Norris, Christopher, 68–71, 73, 76

North, Oliver, 108, 111

Norway, 22

Not Guilty: Report of the Commission of Inquiry into the Charges Made against Leon Trotsky in the Moscow Trials, 22

Novick, Peter, 5, 6; That Noble Dream: The Objectivity Question and the American Historical Profession, 5

Objectivity, 32, 33, 51, 69, 72, 103, 104, 113, 117, 119, 135 (n. 19); historical, 2, 4, 6, 8, 9, 12, 27, 32, 118

Oslo, 21, 22, 24–26, 29, 32

Péguy, Charles, 45, 47, 54, 69, 70, 79; Notre Jeunesse, 45

Perloff, Marjorie, 82

Pétain, Philippe, 85

Picquart, Georges, 36, 43, 54

Poggioli, R., 123

Popular Front, 19, 33

Porch, Douglas, 43

Positivism, 117

Postmodernism, 71, 76, 94, 101, 115, 134 (n. 11)

Pragmatism, 3, 10, 11, 18, 41, 55, 103, 110, 111, 119, 120

Proust, Marcel, 49, 56, 74

Putnam, Hilary, 117–18

Pyatakov, G. L., 13, 21, 22, 24–26, 29, 31, 33

Radek, K., 13, 21

Rationalism, 51, 54

Rationality, 35, 73, 104, 114, 117, 118, 154 (n. 19)

Reader's Digest, 108–9

Reagan, Ronald, 11, 119; and the trip to Bitburg, 11; and defense of trip to Bitburg, 97–115 passim; criticism of, 98, 100, 102, 106; defense of, 103, 107–10, 112, 114, 115; mendacity of, 105, 106–8, 111, 113, 114, 117

Rebatet, Lucien, 82; Les décombres, 82

Regan, Donald, 108

Reinach, Joseph, 54

Relativism, 34, 57; historical, 3

Religion, 7, 8

Rennes, trial at, 38

Rescher, Nicholas, 22

Responses: On Paul de Man's Wartime Journalism, 64, 80, 83, 88

Reville, Albert, 53

Revue des Deux Mondes, 47

Ridgeway, Matthew (General), 100

Rochefort, Henri, 53

Rolland, Romain, 53

Romm, V., 21, 26, 31

Roosevelt, Franklin Delano, 105

Rorty, Richard, 5, 7, 16, 27, 56, 118

Rosenau, Pauline Marie, 71

Rosengoltz, A. P., 13

Roth, Michael, 120

Rubenstein, Diane, 111, 112

Ruehle, Otto, 17

Russian Revolution, 13

Rykov, A., 13, 14

Saturday Evening Post, 105

Scheurer-Kestner, C. A., 37

Schultz, George, 99, 108, 112

Schuman, F. L., 25, 26, 33

Scott, Joan W., 5, 67, 119

Sedov, L. L., 21, 24, 27